From Ameche to Zozzled

A Glossary of Hard-Boiled Slang of the 1920s through the 1940s

From Ameche to Zozzled

A Glossary of Hard-Boiled Slang of the 1920s through the 1940s

PLUS a compendium of dames, detectives, novels, writers, music, and movies!

Joe Tradii

Wise Guy Publishing

© 2018 by Joe Tradii. All rights reserved.

Published by Wise Guy Publishing

Except as permitted under the Unites States Copyright Act of 1976, no part of this publication may be reproduced or distributed in any form or by any means, or stored in a database or retrieval systems, without the prior written permission of the publisher.

Every effort has been made to trace the copyright holders and obtain permission to reproduce any copyrighted material. Any omission will be corrected in later editions.

ISBN: 9781983347450

Contents

Introduction vii

Dictionary 1

Thesaurus 69

Appendix One – The Dozens:

   12 Noteworthy Noir Novels 75
   12 Trendsetting Gumshoes 80
   12 Hard-Boiled Ink Slingers 85

Appendix Two – Fabulous Femme Fatales 87

Appendix Three – Songs & Musical Artists Playlist 101

Appendix Four – A Film Noir Binge-Watch Queue 105

End Notes 108

INTRODUCTION

Who doesn't get a kick out of listening to a character spout off some hard-boiled lingo in a movie or play? There's something undeniably appealing about hearing this patois from the past with its colorful, inventive metaphors and distinctive delivery.

America in particular has always had a fascination with the mobster lexicon and its unique idioms. Beginning in the early 20th century this vernacular began to work its way into the popular culture. Reporters, filmmakers and fiction writers alike embraced this vibrant language spoken by this fascinating, insular, underworld society.

We celebrate this language today through our continued veneration of film noir tough guys like Humphrey Bogart, who embodies the lonely, cynical private eye, or hard-boiled writers like Raymond Chandler, who brought a new sense of style to his characters' speech. Even the comedically acrobatic language of Damon Runyon echoes today, with the adjective "Runyonesque" used to describe flowery, overly-formal, tense-tortured, and often unknowingly ironic language, such as: "Now most any doll on Broadway will be very glad indeed to have Handsome Jack Madigan give her a tumble."

Indeed, one of the most enduringly popular episodes of the original Star Trek TV series finds Captain Kirk and Mr. Spock in a gangster-run simulacrum of Roaring '20s Chicago. It's impossible not to smile hearing the normally taciturn Spock talking out of the side of his mouth with utterances such as "I wood advize youz ta keep dialin'."

People of all stripes continue to enjoy hearing, reading, and coloring their own conversations with the occasional mot noire.

The impetus for this book came about when I looked, unsuccessfully, for a single repository where I could peruse this lingo at my leisure. So I sat about gathering some of my favorite hard-boiled words and idioms, and things just kind of snowballed from there.

This collection is organized into several sections.

First is a straightforward dictionary, with definitions and some usage examples. Don't be shocked when you find a few epithets of the era in there – we're being true to the vernacular.

Second, there's a thesaurus where you can look up some hard-boiled synonyms for modern terms. If you want more than a dozen colorful ways to reference slugging someone, this is the section to visit.

Finally, just for grins, I've provided some background on a few influential writers, books, characters, films, music – and of course femme fatales – along with a list of some of my personal favorites. It's not an exclusive or exhaustive collection, just my two cents as I sit here slinging ink in front of my word mill, getting spifficated.

So pour yourself a healthy slug of hooch, sit back, and get to reading.

DICTIONARY

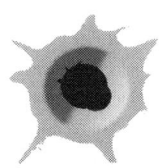
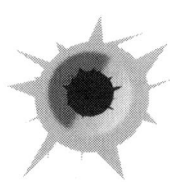
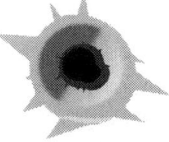

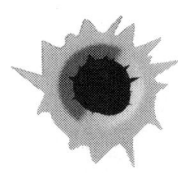

AKA (n) — Name, or assumed name; alias. *"John Miller, AKA Johnny Good Times, AKA John the Jolly, AKA Jackie the knife."*

Alderman (n) — Pot belly. *"Did you get a load of the alderman on that fat-cat mayor?"*

All wet (idiom) — Completely wrong; you don't know what you're talking about. *"I didn't do it and anybody who says different is all wet."*

Altar (n) — Toilet. *"I don't wanna be distoibed – I'll be on the altar."*

Ameche (n) — Telephone. *"Get Joey Nickles on the ameche, I need to talk to him pronto."*

American hashish (n) — Marijuana. *"When he finally showed, he was so gowed up on American hashish he couldn't remember how he got there."*

And how! (intj) — Strongly agree. *"Did you get a load of the gams on that chippy?" "And how!""*

Ankle (n) — Woman. *"Big Eddie has been hanging around with that new ankle from the club."*

Ankle (v) — To walk. *"Listen bub, we're having a private jaw. Why don't you ankle?"*

Ape (n) — Large, oafish man. *"Get outta my office, and take that ape with you."*

Applesauce! (intj) — Baloney, malarkey. *"Aww, applesauce! You cops ain't got nothin' on me."*

Artillery (n) — Handgun or other small arms. *"I'd feel a lot more comfortable if you'd put that artillery back to bed."*

Away at college (idiom) — In prison. *"Lewie the shiv ain't been around for a while. He's away at college."*

B-Girl (n) — 1. Woman employed to chat with customers in a bar while encouraging them to buy drinks. 2. Woman of loose virtue. *"Skids O'Mally went moonface over that new B-Girl and spent all his dough."*

B&E (n) — Breaking and Entering (crime). *"Corky Cavuto just got sent to stoney lonesome for a three spot on a B&E."*

Babe (n) — Woman. *"That babe's so amazing it almost hurts to look at her."*

Baby blues (n) — Eyes. *"Don't cry, it messes up those baby blues."*

Baby grand (n) — Strongly built man. *"So Tommy the Dentist shows up at my place for his money, and he's got this baby grand with him."*

Badger (n) — Femme fatale. Esp. a woman who lures victims of a plot into a compromising or incriminating situation. *"That's the badger that JoJo got mixed up with and ended up going away to college for."*

Bag man (n) — Person who collects ill-gotten money for a crime boss. *"Vinny the Chin needs a new bag man since Mikey got pinched by the bluecoats."*

Balled up (adv) — Messed up. *"The whole caper got all balled up when the guard came back early."*

Bangtail (n) — Racehorse. *"I lost a c-note last Tuesday on that lame bangtail."*

Barber (v) — To converse, especially casually. *"Maybe you have time to stand around and barber but I've gotta see Louie Bagels about a job."*

Bat (n) — Prostitute. *"Stay away from that bat or you'll end up with a case of the clap."*

Bathtub gin (n) — Cheap homemade gin popular during prohibition. *"Crazy Leo got so zozzled on that bathtub gin he almost went blind."*

Bazooms (n) — Woman's breasts. *"The first thing we smart girls learn is that our bazooms are our weapons!"*

Beak (n) — Nose. *"Before I knew it that thug biffed me right on the beak."*

Bean or Pea Shooter (n) — Gun, specifically a handgun. *"Put that pea shooter away before I take it away and beat you with it."*

Bearcat (n) — Fiesty woman. *"Don't mix it up with Velma; that gal's a real bearcat"*

Beat it (v) — Leave. *"Beat it pal; you're not needed here."*

Beat one's gums (idiom) — Useless chatter or idle talk. *"Stop beatin' your gums and get to the point."*

Beau Brummell (n) — A man who takes inordinate interest in his appearance; a dandy. *"That guy's a real Beau Brummell – he spends more time in front of the mirror than the queen in Snow White."*

Bee's knees (adj) — Highly regarded; wonderful. *"My gal think's that Clark Gable guy is just the bee's knees."*

Beezer (n) — Nose. *"I didn't like his attitude so I socked that stooge right in the beezer."*

Behind the eight ball (idiom) — In a jam. *"You gotta front me some scratch; I'm really behind the eight ball."*

Benison (n) — An added bit of luck. *"The moonless night was a benison to my clandestine errand."*

Bent (adj) — Stolen. *"We all went for a joyride in a bent jalopy."*

Bent (adj) — Inebriated. *"Nick the Nail got so bent at that speakeasy, he didn't know which way was up."*

Berries (n) — Dollars. *"I had a few berries in my pocket, a sunny afternoon, and nothing to do but enjoy myself."*

Biff (n) — Punch. *"That mook saw me talking to his gal and biffed me right in the beezer."*

Big cheese (n) — The boss; leader. *"Didn't you know that Fred 'Killer' Burke is the new big cheese of the Purple Gang?"*

Big house (n) — Prison. *"Paddy O'Brien got convicted and sent to the Big House."*

Big six (n) — Strong man. *"You didn't have to send that Big Six over to collect your money, I woulda paid up."*

Big sleep (n) — Death. *"Momo didn't make it. He's in the big sleep."*

Bim (n) — Woman of loose morals. *"She seemed nice at first, but turned out to be a first-class bim."*

Bimbo (n) — A stupid or trashy woman. *"You can always find Sweet Sal accompanied by a couple of bimbos."*

Bindle (n) — The bundle where hobos carried their packages. *"Pack up your bindle and hit the road, ya bum."*

Dictionary

Bindle stiff (n) — Hobo, bum, itinerant. *"He's just a harmless bindle stiff looking for a handout."*

Bing (adv) — Solitary confinement. *"The screws caught Fat Tony with a shiv and threw him in bing."*

Bird (n) — Woman. *"That bird at the bank was a real looker."*

Birds (n) — Generic term for people. *"Okay you birds, fly away. I'm busy."*

Bit (n) — Prison term. *"Like a lot of the gang, Jimmy the Jaw did a bit in the Big House."*

Black and White (n) — Marked police car. *"Last time I went for a ride in a Black and White it cost me $200 for bail."*

Blind Pig (n) — See speakeasy. *"Mustache Pat says there's a new blind pig in town with some first class hooch."*

Blip off (v) — Kill. *"Louie the Knife threatened to blip off anyone who ratted on him."*

Blotto (adv) — Extremely inebriated. *"I don't remember nothin' from last night. I was totally blotto on bathtub gin."*

Blow (v) — 1. To leave, scram. *"The heat's on so I need to blow."* 2. To play a horn instrument. *"That Satchmo sure can blow."*

Blower (n) — Telephone. *"I was just on the blower with Big Sal and he's on the way over."*

Bluecoat (n) — Police officer. *"Sparky Thomas was about to knock over the joint when a bluecoat came along."*

Blue jays (n) — Pills containing sodium amytal, a barbiturate primarily prescribed as a sedative hypnotic. *"You'd have better luck getting a rise out of a stiff than rousing Manny when he's on blue jays."*

Bluenose (n) — Prude. *"That swank restaurant was full of bluenoses."*

Bo (n) — Buddy, friend. *"You can always rely on Big Leo, he's a real bo."*

Bob's your uncle (idiom) — Easy as pie; there you go; simple. *"You tape the dynamite to the safe door, stick in the detonator, get away and Bob's your uncle."*

Bohunk (n) — Derogatory, offensive term for person of central European descent. *"Those bohunks are coming over here and stinking up the neighborhood."*

Boiled (adv) — Inebriated. *"Buddy, after the day I've had I'm getting boiled tonight."*

Boiler (n) — Car. *"He hopped in some boiler and took off before we got a good look at him."*

Bone house (n) — Morgue. *"Itchy Brent heard Crazy Nick was in the bone house."*

Bones (n) — Dice. *"I was throwing bones behind the warehouse with Jake the Weasel all night."*

Boob (n) — Fool; idiot. *"Don't be such a boob."*

Booby hatch (n) — Insane asylum. *"You keep letting that dame mess with you and you'll wind up in the booby hatch"*

Bootleg (n) — Illegal liquor. *"Careful, I heard the latest batch of bootleg will make you blind."*

Boozehound (n) — An alcoholic. *"Everyone knows that Vinny the Chin is an unreliable boozehound."*

Bop (v) — Kill someone. *"When he found out Fingers was a snitch, the Big Cheese wanted to bop him."*

Bounce (v) — To forcibly remove or throw someone out. *"Watch your yap in that gin joint or you'll get bounced."*

Box (n) — Safe. *"Don't worry, the loot is stored in a box in the back room."*

Box job (n) — Crack a safe. *"For this heist we need someone who can pull off a box job."*

Boy-o (n) — Masculine form of address, originally used by the Irish. *"Listen boy-o, it's time to keep your nose out of my business before it gets bent."*

Brace (v) — Interrogate informally; harass; shake up. *"Let me brace him and see what I can find out."*

Bracelets (n) — Handcuffs. *"Before I knew it, the house dick had slapped a pair of bracelets on me."*

Brass (n) — Cash, money. *"Can you front me, I'm short on brass."*

Break it up (idiom) — Stop doing something. *"Break it up you mugs, I can't hear the music."*

Breeze (v) — 1. To leave, scram. *"You better breeze before John Law finds you."* 2. To play a horn instrument. *"That new guy at the Orpheum sure can breeze."*

Breezer (n) — Topless or convertible car. *"I just saw Harry the Hammer on the turnpike in his breezer with some new dame."*

Brittle (adj) — Easily swayed or coerced, often by threats or physical force. *"Let 'em try and get me to sing, I ain't so brittle."* Broad (n) — Woman. *"She was one tough broad, hard to get as an inside straight and just as lucky."*

Brother-in-law (v) — Keep an eye on someone's girl for them. *"Brother-in-lawing for Ed while he's gone, are you?"*

DICTIONARY

Bruiser (n) — Large man working as hired muscle. *"Harry showed up to the meeting with a bruiser in tow."*

Bruno (n) — Tough guy; enforcer. *"Find me a bruno to pay a visit on that deadbeat."*

Bub (n) — Masculine form of address. *"Hey bub, what's your beef?"*

Bubs (n) — Female breasts. *"Knuckles Malloy always was partial to a girl with nice bubs."*

Bucket (n) — Jail. *"The coppers will throw me in the bucket if they catch me breaking parole."*

Bucket (n) — Car. *"That old bucket wouldn't get us to the next corner."*

Buddy (n) — Masculine form of address. *"Hey buddy, can you spare a dime?"*

Bull (n) — Plainclothes cop. *"O'Hara got promoted from a bluecoat to a bull."*

Bum's rush (n) — To be tossed out of a place or unceremoniously asked to leave. *"When Rocko got a little too loud at the bar, the bouncer gave him the bum's rush."*

Bump off (v) — Kill. *"It's easy to bump someone off; it's harder to get away with it."*

Bumper (n) — A drink. *"How about a bumper for the road?"*

Bumpkin (n) — See rube. *"That guy was a real bumpkin, he didn't even know how to hail a hack."*

Bunco; bunco scheme (n) — Scheme meant to defraud. *"Some bull just arrested Jimmy the Gent for running that bunco scheme with kited checks."*

Burn (v) — Kill. *"Big Sal got burned in that shootout last night."*

Burn powder (v) — Fire a gun. *"Get those hands up or I'll burn powder, see."*

Bushwa (interj) — Expression of disbelief. *"Bushwa! You didn't do time at Joliet!"*

Bust (n) — A raid on an illegal establishment or gathering. *"Nobody move, this is a bust!"*

Busted (adj) — 1. Broke. *"I'm so busted I don't even have a thinner."* 2. Arrested. *"Sweet Frank got busted for larceny."*

Buster (n) — Masculine form of address. *"Listen Buster, you better be right about this."*

Butt me (v) — Give me a cigarette. *"Hey Phil, can you butt me?"*

Butter and egg man (n) — The bankroller; the person with the money. *"Once the butter and egg man gets here, we'll have enough dough to buy the dynamite."*

Button (n) — 1. Nose or face. *"That dame had a great figure and cute button."* 2. The police. *"You'd best make yourself scarce before the buttons get here."*

Button man (n) — Hit man or professional killer. *"Vic knew his time was up when he recognized the button man in the front seat."*

Butts (n) — Cigarettes. *"I'm going to the store to pick up some butts and booze."*

Buy the farm (v) — Be killed or die. *"When you see Bruce the button man, you know you're going to buy the farm."*

Buzz (v) — Call by phone or visit in person. *"Give me a buzz next week on the blower."*

Buzzer (n) — Police or detective badge. *"In the sunlight that buzzer on your chest shines like the doorknob on a cathouse."*

C-Note (n) — A hundred-dollar bill. *"The cops found a stack of bogus C-notes in Harry's underwear drawer."*

Cabbage (n) — Money. *"C'mon, show me the cabbage and I'll hand over the dingus."*

Caboose (n) — 1. Jail. *"Freddy the Freeloader got thrown in the caboose for vagrancy."* 2. A woman's rear end. *"Her personality might be lacking, but she's got a great caboose."*

Cagey (adj) — Clever, wary, or suspicious-acting. *"I'm used to stoolies being cagey, but this guy was fit for a zoo."*

Cake-eater (n) — Ladies' man. *"He's had three dates with three different dolls this week; that guy's a real cake eater."*

Can (n) — 1. Bathroom. *"Paulie got pumped full of lead when he was in the can – what a way to go!"* 2. Jail. *"If you don't want to end up in the can you better knock off the five finger discount."* 3. Buttocks. *"I shot him twice in the can as he was running away."*

Can opener (n) — Safe cracker. *"To knock this new bank over we're going to need a top-notch can opener."*

Can-house (n) — Whorehouse. *"The place had a nice feeling even if it was a can-house."*

Canary (n) — 1. An informant. *"The one thing The Boss can't stand is a canary."* 2. A female singer. *"Did you have a chance to listen to that new canary at the nightclub?"*

Canary (v) — To inform on. *"I ain't gonna canary – you can trust me."*

Cancelled stamp (n) — A shy woman; a real downer of a person. *"With her negative personality she was a real cancelled stamp."*

Cannon (or hand-cannon) (n) — Large caliber handgun. *"The bruno had a hand-cannon pointed right at my puss."*

Caper (n) — A robbery or other illicit undertaking. *"From the shifty look in his eyes I could tell he was involved in some kind of caper."*

Carriage trade (n) — Wealthy people, or business conducted with wealthy people. *"You'll never make the carriage trade. You'll always be a cheapie private dick."*

DICTIONARY

Chin music

Carry a torch (idiom) — To continue to have strong feelings and pine for someone after the relationship is over, hence the term *"torch song." "I say the only dame worth carrying a torch for is the Statue of Liberty."*

Castle, The (n) — Sing Sing prison. *"I just graduated after doing a nickel at The Castle."*

Cat's pajamas (idiom) — Phrase meaning something is exemplary or highly desirable. *"With his new racetrack clothes and monkey stick, Diamond Jim went to the club that night feeling like the cat's pajama's and the bee's knees all rolled into one."*

Cement shoes (Also cement slippers or cement overcoat) (n) — Euphemism for being weighted down and drowned. *"That canary is about to get fitted for a pair of cement shoes."*

Century (n) — One hundred dollars. *"Be careful with that coat, it cost me a century."*

Chalk eater (n) — Someone who only places bets on the best odds. Someone who always plays it safe. *"Stop being such a chalk eater and take a chance once in a while."*

Chapeau (n) — Hat. *"I looked very dapper with my new chapeau."*

Cheaters (n) — Eyeglasses. *"Everyone knows Mick the Hammer can't see two feet without his cheaters."*

Cheesed-off (idiom) — Angry. *"I ain't seen Killer Kane so cheesed-off since Squiggy the Squealer ratted him out years ago."*

Cheese it (v) — Hide or quit what you're doing. *"Cheese it, the cops!"*

Chew or chaw (v) — Talk. *"Maybe you should stop chawing and show me what you mean."*

Chicago lightning (n) — Gunfire, specifically automatic gunfire. *"I was startled out of my much-needed sleep by some Chicago lightning outside my window."*

Chicago overcoat (n) — Coffin. *"How'd you like to end up in a Chicago overcoat?"*

Chick or chickie (n) — Woman. *"Joey Jeepers has some new chickie he can't shut up about."*

Chilled off (adv) — Killed. *"From the look on the torpedo's face, I thought I was about to get chilled off."*

Chin (v) — Talk. *"Sounds interesting, let's chin some more about it later."*

Chin music (n) — A punch on the jaw. *"One guy held me while the other thug played chin music on my mug."*

DICTIONARY

Chinese angle (n) — An unusual or unforeseen twist to a situation or problem. *"So your butter and egg man is actually Mr. Big's moll – I thought there was a Chinese angle."*

Chinese squeeze (n) — Skimming money. *"If you keep giving Tony's betting operation the Chinese squeeze you're going to end up with a cement overcoat."*

Chink (n) — Derogatory term for a person of Chinese descent. *"Boy those Chinks make good chow."*

Chippie (n) — Woman (often cheap or loose). *"Forget about that chippie at the bar and focus on the job."*

Chisel (v) — Cheat someone. *"Hey, are you trying to chisel me!?"*

Chisler (n) — A cheater or grifter, someone who doesn't pay or do what they've promised. *"Don't go into business with Slugs McBride; everyone knows he's a chisler."*

Chiv (n) (see also, shiv) — A knife. *"Sparks D'Angelo got it in the back with a chiv while he was in stir."*

Chop house (n) — Restaurant specializing in meat dishes. *"It wasn't the best meal I'd ever had, but it was a decent enough chop house to take a chippie."*

Chop squad (n) — A group of hitmen with automatic weapons. *"The car screeched to a halt and a chop squad jumped out and aired out Charlie the Cheeseman."*

Chopper (n) — Machine gun. *"That chump tried to smuggle a chopper into the can."*

Choppers (n) — Teeth. *"Did you ever get a gander at the choppers on Mick 'The Jaw' Johnson?"*

Chum (n) — Man; masculine form of address. *"Listen chum, I just came here meet a lady – I got no beef with you."*

Chump (n) — See rube. *"Whadaya take me for, a chump?!"*

Chutzpah (n) — Massive self-confidence; nerve. *"It takes a lot of chutzpah to stand up to Jerry the Greek."*

Clam (n) — One dollar. *"Things are rough – I'm down to my last clam."*

Clam juice (n) — Alcoholic beverage. *"Terry's always a lot more of a gas after he's had some clam juice."*

Clam up (v) — Be silent; stop or refuse to speak. *"Don't push him too hard or he'll clam up and we'll never find out where the dough is."*

Clean sneak (n) — An escape or crime that goes off well without leaving any clues. *"That job you pulled was a real clean sneak. The cops have no idea* who did it."

Clap (n) — Venereal disease. *"My big souvenir from my date with that pro skirt was a case of clap."*

Clink (n) — Jail. *"The buttons nabbed me throwing bones and I spent Saturday night in the clink."*

Clip (v) — Kill. *"Crossing Sweet Sal is liable to get you clipped."*

Clip joint (n) — Bar, nightclub, etc. that fleeces its customer by purposefully providing inferior value. *"I thought that new gin mill was on the up and up but it turned out to be a real clip joint."*

Clipped (v) — 1. To be cheated or fleeced. *"Flattop Finnegan got clipped at that back-alley dice game."* 2. To be shot. *"He tried to scram but got clipped in the leg."*

Clout (n) — Shoplifter. *"Marnie was the best clout I ever saw. She could lift a dozen necklaces from the same store."*

Clout (v) — Punch. *"He suckered me with a clout right in the beezer."*

Coconut (n) — Head. *"The piano fell two stories and got poor Sluggo right in the coconut."*

Cold storage (n) — Morgue. *"By the time the reporters arrived the stiff had been shipped off to cold storage."*

Collared (v) — Caught by the authorities. *"Cat-lick Cooper got collared right outside his flop."*

Con (n) — 1. A fraud scheme. *"It could be on the up and up or it could be a clever con."* 2. Someone who has served a prison term. *"No one's going to trust a con with a night watchman job."*

Con (v) — To defraud someone. *"Don't try and con me, I've seen it all."*

Con man (n) — *"Confidence"* man – a swindler or cheat. *"Sweaty Eddie was the worst con man I'd ever seen."*

Cookie (n) — Woman. *"Boy that's one sweet cookie headed this way."*

Cookie-puss (n) — Term of endearment – can also be used sarcastically. *"Aww, don't be mad cookie-puss."*

Cool it (v) — 1. Hide or quit what you're doing. *"Cool it, here comes the guard."* 2. Relax. *"Think I'll just cool it here for a while."*

Cooler (n) — Jail. *"Just my luck I end up in the cooler on my birthday."*

Coop (n) — Any place, e.g. a restaurant, bar, home, etc. See Joint. *"Lets us remove ourselves from this coop and finds a classier joint to patronize."*

Cop (n) — 1. Steal. *"I'd think twice before I tried to cop that ice."* 2. Police officer. *"If you don't like it why don't you call a cop."* 3. Plea or admit to something, often in exchange for a lighter sentence. *"Freddy agreed to cop to the heist."*

Copper (n) — Police officer. *"Come and get me, Copper!"*

Cosa Nostra (n) — Mafia, see also Mob. *"Vito said there's no such thing as the Cosa Nostra, and anyone who thinks different will end up with cement shoes."*

Cough up (idiom) — To talk, or otherwise provide details about something. *"The cops leaned on Little Mo to cough up about the McGillicuddy heist, but he kept his trap shut."*

Crab (v) — To figure something out. *"I finally crabbed what his Chinese angle was."*

Crackers (adj) — Crazy, nuts, bonkers. *"You'd have to be crackers to try and cross Eddie 'The Dentist.'"*

Crate (n) — Car. *"Smitty, trade that old crate in for a newer ride."*

Crazy (adj) — Great, nice. *"That's crazy, sweetheart!"*

Creampuff (n) — A weak, easily cowed, or effeminate man. *"Only a creampuff would canary at the mere suggestion of making the acquaintance of some knuckle dusters."*

Creep Joint (n) — 1. Seedy nightclub. *"A classy dame like Velma wouldn't be caught dead in a creep joint like that."* 2. Disreputable whorehouse. *"Waxey Malone caught the clap at that lousy creep joint."*

Croak (v) — 1. Die. *"If you don't get me to a sawbones soon I'm gonna croak."* 2. Kill. *"Move so much as a finger and I'll croak ya!"*

Croaker (n) — Doctor. *"Louie Bagels was hurt bad, but the only croaker we could find at two in the morning wouldn't come cheap."*

Crocked (v) — 1. Inebriated. *"After the week I've had, I'm looking forward to getting good and crocked."* 2. Hit hard on the head; rendered unconscious. *"Some goon crocked me and the next thing I remember I woke up in an alley."*

Crone (n) — Old woman. *"That crone who runs the boarding house is uglier than Nicky the Nose after a three-day bender."*

Crown (v) — Hit someone very hard, often resulting in unconsciousness. *"One of 'em crowned me and I didn't wake up until a coupla hours after."*

Crush out (v) — Escape, especially from incarceration. *"Mickey crushed out of the Federal Pen in Leavenworth last month."*

Cush (n) — Money safety net. *"Pay me next week, I've got a cush."*

DICTIONARY

Dinge

Dago (n) — Derogatory term for a person of Italian descent. *"Don't let Moonface Morelli hear you call him a dago if you know what's good for you."*

Dago red (n) — Homemade red wine served in cheap Italian restaurants. *"After a plate of spaghetti and some dago red, Chi-Chi the Pyro was feeling pretty good."*

Daisy (n) — Homosexual. *"That's it, you two daisies out of my bar."*

Dame (n) — Woman. *"You don't find a more classy dame than Jessica."*

Darb (adj) — Superior. *"That new watch of yours is real darb."*

Dead drunk (adj) — Extremely inebriated. *"The difference between drunk and dead drunk is that when you're dead drunk you can't even remember the fun you had getting there."*

Deck (n) — Pack of cigarettes. *"I stopped by the liquor store to pick up a pint of Old Harper's and a deck."*

Deck (v) — Hit or punch. *"Why I oughtta deck you for sayin' that about my ma!"*

Deep freeze (n) — Morgue. *"Keep that talk up and you're likely to end up in the deep freeze."*

Derrick (n) — Shoplifter. *"Pippy Cooper's tiny hands made him a great derrick."*

Dewdropper (n) — Unemployed man who spends his days sleeping; a bum. *"Tommy Two Toes has been a real dewdropper since he got out of stir."*

Dibs (n) — Share of the loot. *"Be cool, you'll get your dibs when the heat lets up."*

Dick (n) — Detective. *"That new dick at the precinct came sniffing around looking for Crazy Nick."*

Dinero (n) — Money. *"I'd like to help, but I'm fresh out of dinero."*

Dinge (n) — Derogatory term for African American during the 20s-40s. *"This dinge told me about a great new joint to hear some jazz."*

Dictionary

Dingus (n) — Thing or object. *"Did you ever find that dingus you were looking for yesterday?"*

Dip (n) — Pickpocket. *"To make a good dip, you gotta have nerves of steel."*

Dip the bill (v) — Have a drink. *"Think I'll stop by Smitty's and dip the bill before heading home."*

Dirt nap (n) — Death. *"For all I knew, Squeaky was taking a dirt nap when he missed our appointment."*

Dish (adj) — Pretty; handsome. *"You're the most dish dame I ever saw."*

Dish (n) — Good looking woman. *"I wish I had a rich dish like Benji the Face does."*

Dish (v) — To talk; provide information. *"I can tell you're just itching to tell me something, so c'mon and dish already."*

Dive (n) — Run-down place, such as a bar, restaurant, hotel or apartment. *"Torchy's was a favorite dive for anyone wanting to keep a low profile."*

Dizzy (adj) — 1. In love. *"Let me guess, you're dizzy for that dame."* 2. Stupid. *"Don't be dizzy, I'd never light a match around dynamite."*

Do the Lindy (idiom) — To dance. *"What say you and me go do the lindy tonight?"*

Doghouse (n) — Bass guitar. *"He didn't sing much but he knew how to use that doghouse."*

Dogs (n) — Feet. *"I walked from one side of town to the other and my dogs are barking!"*

Doll (n) — Woman. *"Cathy was one swell doll."*

Doll face (n) — Affectionate form of address for a woman. *"How ya doin', doll-face?"*

Don't get your gauge up (idiom) — Don't get excited. *"You'll get your dibs, don't get your gauge up."*

Don't know from nothing (idiom) — Doesn't have any information. *"When it comes to who knocked over that bank, I don't know from nothin'."*

Don't take any wooden nickels (idiom) — Casual goodbye; don't do anything stupid. *"See you next week. In the meantime, don't take any wooden nickels."*

Dope (n) — 1. Stupid person. *"That bumpkin was a real dope."* 2. Information. *"You'd better give him the dope if you don't want to get roughed up."* 3. Drugs. *"When Charlie's on dope, he's no good to be around."*

Doss (n) — Prostitute. *"If you ask me, she's just a doss."*

Doss (v) — 1. To sleep in a temporary place. *"Know any good places to doss around here?" 2. To have sex for money. *"Maybe she's being so nice because she wants to doss."*

Double sawbuck (n) — A twenty-dollar bill. *"When I give a stoolie a double sawbuck I expect more information than just the color of a guy's hair."*

Dough (n) — Money. *"I spent the last of my dough on that doss."*

Doxy (n) — Prostitute. *"His assumption she was a doxy earned him a slap in the puss from her."*

Drift (v) — Leave. *"I got nothin' to say to you, chum. Drift."*

Drill (v) — Shoot. *"That chippie's jealous husband drilled Charlie last night."*

Drip (n) — Fool, idiot, or spoilsport. *"If you don't show up at the party, everyone will think you're a real drip."*

Drop a nickel (Idiom) — 1. To inform on someone. 2. Literally, to make a phone call. *"You'd best be moving along before one of those so-called friends drops a nickel on you."*

Dropper (n) — Hit man or professional killer. *"I could tell by the look in his eye and the bulge in his jacket the guy was a dropper."*

Drum (n) — Speakeasy. *"We should dip our bills at the new drum."*

Dry up (v) — Shut up; get lost. *"If you know what's good for you, you'll dry up."*

Ducat (n) — Ticket. *"Nobody gets into the game without a ducat."*

Ducats (n) — Dollars, money. *"I've got the ducats to pay the bill."*

Duck soup (adj) — Easy; a piece of cake. *"Knocking over that bodega that didn't have any locks was duck soup."*

Dude (n) — Fastidious man; dandy. *"Whoe's the dude with the spats and diamond cufflinks?"*

Dull (adj) — Dimwitted; not too bright. *"I don't want to say that Luca is dull, but he's definitely not the sharpest knife in the drawer."*

Dumb bunny (n) — Foolish or stupid person. *"Of course she's a doxy, you dumb bunny."*

Dumb Dora (n) — Stupid person. *"Don't be such a dumb Dora."*

Dummy up (idiom) — Shut up; be quiet. *"Dummy up before I drill ya."*

Dump (n) — See dive. *"I wouldn't be caught dead in that dump."*

Dupe (n) — See patsy. *"Now the only thing we need is a dupe to take the rap."*

Dust (v) — Leave. *"We're talking business, so dust, buddy."*

Dictionary

Dutch

Dutch (adv, n) — 1. (In) trouble. *"I can't go home, I'm in dutch with the missus."* 2. Suicide. *"Looks more like a dutch than a murder to me."*

Dutch Uncle (n) — Someone who sternly advises or admonishes you. *"The last thing he needed right now was anyone acting like a Dutch Uncle."*

Eel juice (n) — Liquor. *"I'll feel better after I've got some eel juice in me."*

Egg (n) — Person living the good life. *"I'm not some egg who was born with a silver spoon."*

Egg in your beer (idiom) — Something extra that adds no value. Something for nothing. *"What do you want, an egg in your beer?"*

Eggs in the Coffee (idiom) — Everything is excellent, wonderful, ideal. *"My new car is really eggs in the coffee compared to that last junker I owned."*

Eighty-Six (v) — Get rid of something or someone. *"Let's eighty-six this slop and get some decent chow."*

Electric cure (n) — Execution by electrocution. *"Mickey went up to Sing Sing and got the electric cure."*

End, or My End (n) — Cut of the loot. *"Just make sure when it's over that I get my end."*

Enforcer (n) — Hired thug. *"No need to send an enforcer, I'll cooperate."*

Erase (v) — Kill someone. *"Maybe instead of letting you go I'll just erase you instead."*

Ethel (n) — Effeminate male. *"Get a load of the Ethel that just minced in here."*

Ex-nay (idiom) — To stop something. *"Sideways Sal put the ex-nay on bringing any more loogans into the outfit."*

Dictionary

Fade (v) — Go away; get lost. *"Why don't you fade while we talk business."*

Fairy (n) — Homosexual. *"Did someone make you wear that shirt, or are you just a fairy?"*

Fakeloo artist (n) — See con man. *"Why would I trust you? For all I know you're a fakeloo artist."*

Fall guy (n) — Someone set up to take the blame for a crime. *"To take the heat off us after this caper we need a fall guy."*

Fan (v) — Search for something. *"Fan the room boys, the dingus has to be here somewhere."*

Fat City (n) — An ideal situation; an enviable state of affairs. *"With your new gal and big promotion, you're in fat city."*

Fella (m) — Man. *"Calm down fella, no need to get your gauge up."*

Fill full of daylight (idiom) — To shoot repeatedly. *"They opened up with their choppers and filled him full of daylight."*

Fin (n) — A five dollar bill. *"Loan me a fin, I've got a tip on a bangtail."*

Finger (v) — To identify someone. *"I think Manny Malloy put the finger on me for that job in Rochester."*

Finger man (n) — Snitch; inside person. *"We need to find who the finger man is that ratted us out."*

Fink (n) — An informant. *"Lefty Leroy will never tell the cops. He's no fink."*

Fish (n) — 1. First-timer in prison. *"Who's the new fish in cellblock A?"* 2. One dollar. *"I don't even have a single fish to my name."*

Fishbowl (n) — Holding cell at the police station. *"They held me in the fishbowl all weekend but let me go Monday after my mouthpiece showed up."*

Five-finger discount (n) — Shoplifting. *"Bugsy was showing off his new watch he got with a five-finger discount."*

Five-spot (n) — 1. Five-year term in jail. *"Mustache Mike is doing a five spot in Joliet because of some fink."* 2. A five-dollar bill. *"I gave the sallow-faced* bellhop a five-spot and sent him to fetch the evening paper and a pint of Old Grand-dad."

Flag (v) — To send for or to pay a visit to. *"You stay put while I go flag our butter and egg man."*

Flat (adj) — Broke; having no money. *"Don't look at me for a loan – I'm flat."*

Flat tire (n) — Boring or uninteresting person. *"You can be a real flat tire sometimes."*

Flatfoot (n) — Police officer, specifically one who walks a beat. *"A dip can't work this street any more with that new flatfoot always watching."*

Fleece (v) — To take money from unfairly; to grift. *"Joining Buck's rigged card game is a good way to get fleeced."*

Flim-flam (v) — To cheat someone. *"Are you trying to flim-flam me with some scheme?"*

Flim-flam man (n) — See con man. *"Every good flim-flam man knows the three card monte."*

Flipped (v) — 1. Went crazy; lost control. *"Nicky Nails saw his dame with another fella and just flipped."* 2. Turned on someone and informed the police. *"Everything was jake until one of the gang was picked up by the cops and flipped."*

Flipped his/her wig (idiom) — Lost control, usually in anger. *"Stumpy found out someone ratted on him and flipped his wig."*

Flivver (n) — A cheap car, especially one in bad condition. *"That flivver won't make it to the end of the block, much less to Toledo."*

Floater (n) — A corpse found in a body of water. *"I hear the buttons found a floater in Rattlesnake Lake this morning."*

Flogger (n) — Overcoat. *"You better take your flogger, it looks cold outside."*

Floozy (n) — Cheap or loose woman. *"If I want a roll in the hay, I'll find a floozy."*

Flop (v) — Sleep for free; stay overnight. *"Mind if I flop here tonight?"*

Flophouse (n) — A cheap and filthy hotel, often frequented by vagrants. *"Floozies frequently frequent flophouses."*

Fog (v) — Shoot. *"Come out where I can see you or I'll fog you."*

Foghorn (n) — Tuba. *"If I were going to be in a marching band, the foghorn is the last instrument I'd pick."*

Folded (v) — Closed for the night, as a bar or restaurant. *"After the bar folded at midnight we found an all-night dive."*

DICTIONARY

Follow the Lady (n) — Confidence game where marks pay money to guess which card is the Queen. Also called Three-card Monte. *"I can't believe Louie the Lip lost a century playing Follow the Lady."*

Four-flusher (n) — Person who feigns wealth while mooching off others. *"I thought he was a real egg but it turned out he was only a four-flusher."*

Frail (n) — Woman. *"Minnie was a tough frail, but had a heart as big as a whale."*

Frau (n) — Wife. *"No more for me, I have to be getting back to the frau."*

Frisk (v) — Search a person or place. *"If you didn't ice Pete the Pistol, then you won't mind if I frisk you for a shiv."*

Frowst (n) — A stuffy, stale, musty, or offensive odor. *"The dive had the usual frowst – stale beer, sweat, the pungent scent of lingering desperation."*

Fry (v) — Execute by electrocution. *"If he's convicted of airing out that fink he'll fry for sure."*

Funny house (n) — Insane asylum. *"She drove him to bankruptcy, then she drove him to the funny house."*

G-Man, or G-Boy (n) — Government agent. *"You don't want Melvin the G-Man on your case."*

Gaffer (n) — Old man. *"Nobody lives in that flophouse but gaffers and crones."*

Galoot (n) — Large, oafish man. *"Take your hands off me, you big galoot."*

Gams (n) — Woman's legs. *"She had a set of gams that went from here to there, transferred, and kept on going."*

Gargle (v) — Have a drink. *"I don't know about you, but after a day like today I could use a good gargle."*

Gashouse district (n) — Run-down district of a city, often a haunt of gangsters. *"Even Frankie the Nose won't go down to the gashouse district after midnight."*

Gaslight (v) — Sow seeds of doubt in a person about their memory or sanity, i.e. mess with their head. *"Stop making things up – you're just tryin' to gaslight me."*

Gasper (n) — Cigarette. *"As I watched her walk away into the stygian night, I felt inside my coat for my last gasper."*

Gat (n) — Handgun. *"Suppose you put that gat away and we talk about this."*

Gaycat (n) — Young homosexual often associated with an older man. *"That gaycat Toby never gets too far from that old gaffer."*

Geetus (n) — Money. *"Show me the geetus right now or there's gonna be trouble."*

Geezer (n) — Old man. *"We look like a couple of geezers sittin' on this bench."*

George (n) — Any Pullman porter. *"I need help with these bags, go and find George."* Or, *"Let George do it."*

George Eddy (n) — Cheap tipper. *"I left the floozy at the chop house a tip she hadn't earned and plunged into the night. I might be a lot of things, but I'm no George Eddy."*

Get a wiggle on! (idiom) — Get going. *"Hey toots, get a wiggle on or we'll be late."*

Get in a lather (idiom) — Become angry or agitated. *"Never let Crazy Eddie know how goofy he looks when he gets in a lather."*

Get wise (v) — 1. Act smart-alecky. *"Don't get wise with me, junior."* 2. Obtain information. *"Alrgiht, get wise on the new G-Man and report back."*

Getaway sticks (n) — Woman's legs. *"As a connoisseur of gams, I can attest this dame had a pair of getaway sticks that nobody would run away from."*

Giggle Juice (n) — Liquor. *"Shut up and make with the giggle juice – I'm parched."*

Gimcrack (n) — Cheap, flashy object often of little value. *"That girlie has more gimcracks and geegaws than a novelty store."*

Gimmick (n) — Angle, scheme, trick. *"Sounds too good to be true, so what's your gimmick?"*

Gin Mill (or Gin joint) (n) — Bar or nightclub. *"Of all the gin mills she had to walk into mine."*

Ginzo (n) — Pejorative term for a person of Italian heritage. *"If you're going to ginzo-town, bring me back a couple bottles of dago red."*

Girlie (n) — Woman. *"Take it easy girlie, no one is going to hurt a hair on your head."*

Git Box (n) — Guitar. *"He could play the git box like nobody."*

Give (v) — Talk, provide details about something. *"I know you know where Fat Tony's been hiding out, so give."*

Give it to him (idiom) — Shoot someone. *"He pulled a shiv on me so I had to give it to him."*

Give the Third (Degree) (idiom) — Interrogate; question closely. *"Stop giving me the third degree, I don't know nothin'"*

Give up the ghost (idiom) — To die. *"After complaining about his heart for years, Sanford finally gave up the ghost."*

Glad rags (n) — Fancy, dress clothes. *"Put on your glad rags, we're going uptown."*

Glom (v) — 1. Steal. *"That dipper just glommed my wallet."* 2. Grab hold of or hold closely. *"Did you see the way he glommed onto her all night?"*

Go climb up your thumb (interj) — Get lost, scram, go F yourself. *"Why don't you go climb up your thumb, pal."*

Gob (n) — Mouth. *"No one's talking to you so shut your gob."*

Gone over (idiom) — Beaten up. *"The flatfoots found him lyin' in the alley after he'd been gone over pretty good."*

Dictionary

Green

Gonif (n) — Thief (literally or figuratively). *"Could you believe how much that gonif wanted for that old jalopy?"*

Goods (The) (n) — The subject or subjects in question. *"The coppers wanted me to give up the goods on Crazy Eddie, but I stonewalled."*

Goofball (n) — Barbiturate mixed with Benzedrine for illegal use. *"Keep popping those goofballs and you'll end up dead or in the Funny House."*

Goofy (adv) — Crazy; stupid. *"Don't get goofy over every chippie that walks in the door."*

Goofy juice (n) — Alcohol. *"Sammy, set me up with some goofy juice."*

Goog (n) — Black eye. *"Nice goog. How's the other guy?"*

Goombah (n) — A person of Italian descent or sometimes a member of an organized criminal outfit. *"C'mere and gimme a hug, you big goombah."*

Goon (n) — Thug. *"Zeppo came by to collect his vig and brought along a couple of goons."*

Goose (n) — Person. *"Stop being a goofy goose."*

Gooseberry lay (v) — Steal clothing off a clothesline. *"That hobo's on the gooseberry lay."*

Gorilla (n) — Hired thug. *"Who's the new gorilla Slammin' Sam has working for him?"*

Gowed up (adj) — High on drugs. *"He was so gowed up, he didn't know what planet he was on."*

Grab some air (idiom) — Put your hands up (usually at gunpoint). *"Grab some air or I'll drill the next wiseacre opens his gob."*

Graduate (n) — Get out of prison. *"Why would Tony TaTa break out of stir when he was about to graduate?"*

Graft (n) — A cut of the take from illegal activity. *"Looks like the mayor got caught in a graft scandal."*

Grand (n) — One thousand dollars. *"Thanks to some lousy bangtail I'm into Bones Barbini for five grand."*

Greaser (n) — Pejorative for a Mexican person. *"Do you know that greaser who started working at Big Sal's?"*

Greasy spoon (n) — Cheap diner or restaurant, often of inferior quality. *"I'd been in my share of greasy spoons, but calling this joint a greasy spoon would be an insult to greasy spoons."*

Green (n) — Money. *"You show me the green, I'll show you the goods."*

Dictionary

Grift

Grift (n) — A confidence game or scheme. *"What kind of grift are you running with those fake IDs anyway?"*

Grifter (n) — See con man. *"Pinky Carruth got taken to the bank by that grifter in a beautiful sting."*

Grill (v) — Question intently. *"Listen you mug, either spill or we'll take you to the station and grill you."*

Groan-Box (n) — Accordion. *"I pulled out my harmonica and JJ got his groan box and together we played into the wee hours."*

Grummy (adj) — Depressed. *"Tommy Perfect was pretty grummy after his gal tossed him for some sheik."*

Guff (n) — Useless or cheeky talk. *"Any more guff out of you and you'll get a knuckle sandwich."*

Guinea (n) — Pejorative term for an Italian person. *"Say what you want about that Guinea Guido, but he makes a mean meatball."*

Gum up (adv) — Mess up. *"I swear if you gum this up, I'll plug you."*

Gumshoe (n) — Detective. *"No two-bit gumshoe is going to slap any nippers on me."*

Gun for someone (idiom) — Hunt a person; have it out for someone. *"Ever since I took Tommy Perfect's dame he's been gunning for me."*

Gun holder (n) — Hired gunman (often temporary or for a single job.) *"With a reputation as a hopeless souse, Lenny's days as a gun holder were over."*

Gunpoke (n) — Hired gunman. *"If you think a couple of itchy gunpokes can intimidate me, you're probably right."*

Gunsel (n) — Mobster or criminal carrying a gun, usually working for another mobster or criminal; thug. *"Tell that gunsel to put that piece away or he'll be breathing out of his ears."*

Hack (n) — Taxi. "*I went outside to catch a ride home but there wasn't a hack in sight.*"

Half (n) — A fifty cent piece. "*I'll bet you this half that you can't guess where Bucky Bones is sleeping tonight.*"

Half under (adj) — Very inebriated. "*I was so blotto i didn't know if I was half-under or completely submerged.*"

Half-seas over (adj) — Very inebriated. "*The boys really tied one on last night, every single one was half-seas over by nine o'clock.*"

Hard-boiled (adj) — Tough; cynical. "*She might have been a soft touch, but her manager was one hard-boiled character.*"

Hardware/piece of hardware (n) — Gun. "*If we're going up against the Bambino Family, you had better bring some heavy duty hardware.*"

Harlem sunset (n) — Knife wound from a fight, often fatal. "*This wasn't the work of some punk carving Harlem sunsets on some poor shmoe – this was a pro.*"

Harness bull (n) — Street cop in uniform. "*The harness bull on the sidewalk didn't notice as I ducked into the alley.*"

Harp (n) — Person of Irish descent. "*Don't worry about Finnegan, he's a harmless old Harp.*"

Hash house (n) — Cheap diner or restaurant. "*I saw Joey Five Cents eating at that new hash house on Maple yesterday morning.*"

Have your ticket punched (idiom) — Be killed. "*I kept one eye on the door and one hand on the roscoe in my pocket; I had no intention of having my ticket punched tonight.*"

Hayburner (n) — Horse one loses money on. "*Michaleen Flynn can always spot a hayburner. Unfortunately, it's usually the bangtail he's betting on.*"

Haymaker (n) — Solid, knockout punch. "*Suddenly the sky was full of stars as the goon laid a haymaker on me.*"

Heater (n) — Handgun. "*What's a nice doll like you doing with a heater stuffed in her girdle?*"

DICTIONARY

Heebie-jeebies (n) — Shaking from fright or withdrawal. *"I get the heebie-jeebies just thinking about eating in that greasy spoon."*

Heeled (adj) — Carrying a gun. *"Nothing to worry about, I'm heeled."*

Heister (n) — Thief, criminal. *"You're not some slick operator; you're a cheap heister and you'll always be a cheap heister."*

Hellcat (n) — A fiery or vengeful woman, often given to violence. *"You don't want to cross that dame; she's a real hellcat."*

Het up (adj) — Angry or agitated. *"Marco is all het up over something."*

Hides (n) — Drums. *"They call him sticks' because he's a genius on the hides."*

High-hat (n) — Snobbish person. *"Did that high-hat just make fun of my spats?"*

His name is Denis (idiom) — He's done for; he's a goner. *"If she gave me away, my name is Denis."*

Hit (v) — Kill on someone's orders. *"Bugsy just put out a hit on Fearless Frankie."*

Hitman (n) — A hired contract killer. *"Judging by the way you tore into that steak, you can always get work as a professional hitman."*

Hit the road (idiom) — Leave the scene. *"The bluecoats will be here soon so hit the road."*

Hobo (n) — Itinerant worker or vagrant who often stole rides on trains from town to town. *"Hobos have their own language when they're on the road."*

Hock (v) — To pawn something. *"Six-string Stu was heartbroken when he had to hock his guitar."*

Hooch (n) — Alcohol, usually cheap. *"The place wasn't much for atmosphere but the hooch wasn't bad."*

Hoochie-coochie (n) — A provocative belly dance type dance, such as the shimmy. *"Of course I was working; ya think I spent all night doing the hoochie-coochie?!"*

Hood (n) — Thug. *"Frankie has a new hood working for him that's as big as a house!"*

Hooey (n) — Useless or false information or talk; malarkey. *"That's the biggest load of hooey I heard since they said the Saint Valentine's day massacre was a train accident."*

Hoofer (n) — Dancer, either professional or amateur. *"That Fred Astaire is one terrific hoofer."*

Dictionary

Hymie

Hoop (n) — Horse jockey. "*Last I heard, Shorty was running a grift with a crooked hoop at Santa Anita.*"

Horse parlor (n) — Establishment to place illegal bets on horse racing. "*Let's visit that horse parlor on 78th and play the ponies tomorrow.*"

Horsefeathers (intj) — Nonsense. Used to express scorn. "*You say you'll have the money by Friday. I say horsefeathers!*"

Hoosegow (n) — Jail. "*Reno and Penny got soused last night and ended up in the hoosegow downtown.*"

Hop-head (n) — Drug addict. "*Never trust a hop-head as a lookout.*"

Horn (n) — Telephone. "*Get Teppo on the horn and tell him the deal's off.*"

Hot dog stand (n) — Disparaging term for a restaurant. "*What say you and I blow this hot dog stand and find a class joint to chow down.*"

House dick (n) — Hotel detective. "*I think the new house dick at the Savoy Hotel used to be a gumshoe in the Third Precinct.*"

Hymie (n) — Pejorative term for a Jewish person. "*That hymie is part of the Kosher Nostra, I hear.*"

I

I have to go see a man about a dog (idiom) — Misleading excuse to surreptitiously leave for another reason, e.g. to go to the racetrack or buy booze. *"I'd love to talk more, but I've got to see a man about a dog."*

Ice (n) — Diamonds. *"That dame was showing more ice than the north pole."*

Ice (v) — Kill. *"A fella who crosses Dirty Dick is likely to get iced."*

Ice house, or ice box (n) — Jail. *"I got picked up for dipping and spent Tuesday night in the icebox."*

Iced to the eyebrows (idiom) — Extremely inebriated. *"What would you know about what happened last night? You were iced to the eyebrows!"*

In cold storage (idiom) — In jail. *"You can either spill about that bank job last week or spend the next few days in cold storage."*

In hock (idiom) — In debt to someone. *"I can't go see Fast Eddie 'cause I'm still in hock to him big time."*

In stir (idiom) — In jail. *"Last I heard, Jimmy Diamond was safely out of the way in stir."*

In the chips (idiom) — Financially well off. *"After we pull this next caper we'll be in the chips."*

Iron (n) — Gun. *"Put that iron away and let's talk like businessmen."*

Ivories (n) — Piano. *"I've been known to tickle the ivories from time to time."*

J

Jack (n) — 1. Money. *"You're going to need a lot of jack to keep a dame like Carina happy."*   2. Man. *"Before I give you the poop, show me the jack, jack."*

Jailbait (n) — An attractive underage girl. *"Given your extremely poor decision making history, I'd avoid that jailbait if I was you."*

Jake (adv) — Okay; good. *"Don't worry about anything, it's all Jake."*

Jalopy (n) — Car, usually run down. *"You're braver than I thought if you drove here in that jalopy."*

Jam (n) — A real mess. *"As usual, Rocky couldn't stay away from the jailbait and wound up in another jam."*

Jamoke (n) — A stupid or inept person; an unsophisticated person. *"What do you two jamokes want now?"*

Jane (n) — Woman. *"She was a fine-looking jane, with smarts to boot."*

Jasper (n) — Someone from the country; a hick. *"That jasper wouldn't know a salad fork from a tuning fork."*

Java (n) — Coffee. *"After getting blotto last night, all I could think about was getting some java in me."*

Jaw (v) — To talk. *"I'd love to stand here and jaw all afternoon, but I've got to see a man about a horse."*

Jerkin (n) — Close-fitting leather men's jacket. *"All's I seen was a tall skinny guy in a jerkin dusting out the back door."*

Jig is up (idiom) — Expression indicating that a plan or subterfuge has been exposed. *"He knows that cabbage is counterfeit – the jig is up!"*

Jim-Jams (n) — The jitters. *"I got the jim-jams 'cause I never knocked over nothing like a bank before."*

Jimmy (n) —To force open a lock, often illegally. *"All I had to do to get the goods on him was to jimmy the door, grab the snaps, and vamoose."*

Jingle-brained (adj) — Not bright; muddled. *"Get that jingle-brained bim out of my sight before she messes anything else up."*

Dictionary

Jitney

Jitney (n) — Taxi. *"On the midnight street there was no limo, no car, not even a jitney in sight."*

Jitterbug (n) — 1. Nervous person. *"What's that jitterbug got the jim-jams about?"* 2. Dance (noun or verb). *"Hey baby, let's jitterbug all night then hit that new gin joint."*

Jive (n) — Double-talk; slang. *"Don't hit me with that jive, I know better."*

Job (n) — A robbery. *"Did you pull that job at the horse parlor where a grifter got squiffed?"*

Joe (n) — 1. Coffee. *"A strong cup of joe and a slice of cherry pie would hit the spot."* 2. Man. *"You can trust Frank, he's a good Joe."*

Joe Brooks (n) — Well-dressed man. *"I heard Big Julie really fell hard for that Joe Brooks at the Imperial."*

John (n) — Customer of a prostitute. *"That pro skirt has more johns than an Irish bar has Seans."*

John Law (n) — A police officer, or the police in general. *"You'll never take me alive, John Law!"*

Johnson Brother (n) — Professional criminal. *"He'd like to think he's a Johnson Brother but he's strictly amateur."*

Joint (n) — 1. Place such as a bar, nightclub, restaurant, etc. *"Last night the joint was really jumpin'"*. 2. Jail or prison. *"After he got busted for hosting dice games, Nathan D. is back in the joint."*

Joss house (n) — Chinese temple or, more generally, a Chinese establishment. *"If you want to relax, visit a Joss House. We've got work to do."*

Joy girl (n) — Prostitute. *"I know Phil's got a favorite joy girl who works on the lower east side."*

Joy house (n) — Bordello. *"You go ahead. I haven't paid a visit to a joy house since my salad days."*

Judy (n) — Woman. *"That judy Charlie was with last night used to work as a torcher downtown."*

Ju-jus (n) — Marijuana cigarettes. *"I can pick up some ju-jus from Sweet Willie and we can forget our troubles."*

Jug (n) — Jail. *"I want to double date with her as much as I want to get tossed back in the jug."*

Juice (n) — 1. The interest on a loan, especially from a loan shark. *"What's the juice that shylock's getting?"* 2. Power or influence. *"Who's got more juice with the boss, me or you?"*

Juice (v) — To bribe someone. *"It's going to take more than you've got to juice that bank manager into giving you the armored truck delivery schedule."*

Juice joint (n) — Speakeasy or cheap bar. *"I stumbled into the nearest juice joint with the somewhat dubious plan to drink my troubles away."*

Junkie (n) — Drug addict. *"You can tell he's a junkie by the needle marks on his arms."*

K

Kabosh (n) — Prevent or say no to something. *"Before I could explain any more details, Johnny put the kabosh on the whole plan."*

Kale (n) — Money. *"Look at all the kale that Beau Brummell's got on him!"*

Kick (n) — Wallet. *"I got a cool two hundred smacks in my kick."*

Kick (n) — A thrill. *"It was a kick watching that gunsel being gone over, but it still left a bad taste in my mouth like stale beer and cheap gin."*

Kick (or Kick off) —Kick (v) — 1. To complain. *"You got your share of the loot so what are you kicking about?"* 2. To die. *"Keep your hands off my girl, I'm not going to kick any time soon."*

Kid (n) — Affectionate term for a woman. *"Here's looking at you, kid."*

Killjoy (n) — Wet blanket; dour person. *"You're a worse killjoy than a Baptist preacher at a burlesque show."*

Kiss (n) — A punch. *"That thug planted a kiss right on my beezer."*

Kiss (v) — To punch. *"If you don't pipe down I'm going to kiss you like you've never been kissed."*

Kisser (n) — Mouth. *"One of these days... Pow! Right in the kisser."*

Kite a check (v) — Engage in check fraud; make use of non-existent funds in a checking or other bank account. *"Willy the Weasel got busted kiting checks and ended up back in stir."*

Kitten (n) — Woman. *"You know you're my number one girl, kitten."*

Knock off (v) — Kill. *"If Tony the Turk knocks off the Sicilian it's going to start a turf war for sure."*

Knock over (v) — Rob; burgle. *"If you think it's so easy to knock over a bank, be my guest."*

Knock up (v) — Impregnate. *"Floozy Flo got knocked up by Sweet Sal and she's keeping the baby."*

Knockers (n) — A woman's breasts. *"She's not much for conversation, but those knockers!"*

Know your onions (idiom) — To comprehend what's going on. *"Come back when you know your onions, then we can talk more."*

Know-nothing (n) — Idiot; fool. *"Just because I'm from Poughkeepsie doesn't mean I'm a know-nothing rube."*

Knuckle duster (n) — Brass knuckles. *"Last time I got kissed with a knuckle duster I lost a couple of teeth."*

Knuckle sandwich (n) — A punch. *"Whitey complained about his old lady's cooking so much she finally served him a knuckle sandwich."*

Knucks (n) — Brass knuckles. *"Before I could say Jack Robinson I was crocked by some knucks the gorilla had slipped on."*

Kosher (adj) — Legitimate. *"Not to worry, this job is 100% kosher."*

Kosher Nostra (n) — The Jewish mafia. *"Solly is very highly placed in the Kosher Nostra, so give him plenty of space."*

L

Lam (v) — On the run. *"After that jewelry store caper I have to go on the lam, so you won't be seeing me for a while."*

Large (n) — A thousand dollars. *"Snake-eyes Smith owes Sky Winters five large after that run of back luck with the bones."*

Lay (n) — Sexual Intercourse. *"All Nico can think about is having a lay with that new waitress."*

Lead pipe cinch (n) — A sure thing. *"Trust me, this horse is a lead pipe cinch to win tomorrow."*

Lead poisoning (n) — To be shot. *"I decided to make myself scarce to avoid a fatal case of lead poisoning."*

Lean on (idiom) — To strongly coerce someone. *"The local bluecoats would lean on him and he'd crack like peanut brittle."*

Legged it (v) — Took off quickly; ran away. *"When Lucky Larry heard the husband's car pull up, he legged it out the back door."*

Legger (n) — A person making and or distributing illegal liquor, especially during 1920s prohibition. Short for bootlegger. *"That legger's car has a least two extra trunks the G-men aren't wise to."*

Let George do it (idiom) — Work evading phrase. *"Take out the trash and don't tell me to let George do it."*

Lettuce (n) — Money. *"How much lettuce do you have on you to bribe this flatfoot?"*

Lick (n) — Punch. *"I managed to get in a few licks before a haymaker from that goon put my lights out."*

Lid (n) — Hat. *"A gentleman removes his lid when indoors."*

Limey (n) — British person. *"Some Limey fresh off the boat is trying to move in on Lou the Lip's territory."*

Lingo (n) — Language or vernacular. *"Translate that for me; I'm not conversant in mobster lingo."*

Lip (n) — 1. Backtalk. *"Shaddup, that's enough lip out of you."* 2. A lawyer. *"Vinny The Shiv beat that rap thanks to some fancy lip he hired."*

Licorice stick (n) — A clarinet. *"Boy that Artie Shaw sure can blow a licorice stick."*

Lit (adj) — Inebriated. *"I could tell this jamoke was lit from his rough-seas stance and the reek of cheap gin."*

Live wire (n) — Entertaining or lively person. *"If you want to raise the roof at your party be sure and invite that live wire Vic the Quick."*

Lizzie lice (n) — Police patrolling in a car. *"Watch your back tonight, Lizzie Lice is out in force."*

Loaded (adj) — 1. Inebriated. *"My gal and I got loaded to the gills on the hooch at that new speakeasy."* 2. Armed. *"If you go into Big Sal's territory better make sure you're loaded."*

Lockup (n) — Holding cell or jail. *"I spent a pleasant weekend in lockup watching a couple of boozehounds sleep it off. It was very entertaining."*

Lollygagger (n) — Idler. *"Don't tell me you're leaning against that wall to hold it up, lollygagger."*

Long drop (The) (n) — To hang. *"The next morning Joey No Nose was scheduled to take the long drop for icing those tourists."*

Loogan (n) — Man with a gun. *"I would say that the roscoe he's holding definitely qualifies him as a loogan."*

Looker (n) — Attractive woman. *"She was a real looker, the kind of woman that hijacks your dreams at night."*

Lookout (n) — A sentry during a crime, ready to give warning to the perpetrators. *"Asking Smitty to hold your cash is like asking a blind man to be your lookout."*

Loot (n) — Money or other ill-gotten gains. *"Where did you hide the loot after that jewelry store heist?"*

Louse (n) — Bum; no-good person. *"In the end, he turned out to be just another two-bit, shiftless, no account louse."*

Lousy Liz (n) — Cheap prostitute. *"The difference between a respectable dame and a Lousy Liz is that you'll spend less money on the hooker, but also come away with the crabs."*

Lousy with (adj) — Rife, bursting with. *"Jack The Clamp called off the bank heist when he saw the lobby was lousy with bluecoats."*

Lubed (adj) — Inebriated. *"By the time we arrived, everyone at the party was pretty well lubed."*

Lug (n) — Brutish man. *"Each new lug Diamonds Nelson hired was bigger and dumber than the last."*

Lush

Lush (n) — An alcoholic. *"Hogarth was such a lush he made the jungle look thirsty."*

M

Mac (n) — Masculine form of address. *"Hey Mac, where can a guy find a good steak in this town?"*

Made man (n) — Mobster who's been formally accepted into a criminal organization. *"With a handshake and a kiss from the Don, I was now a Made Man."*

Mahaska (n) — Gun, specifically a handgun. *"Flatbush Frank pulled out his mahasca and let loose with an impressive spray of lead."*

Make a monkey out of me (idiom) — Cause someone to look foolish. *"Find another fall guy; 'cause you won't make a monkey out of me."*

Make like a statue (idiom) — See Grab some air. *"Make like a statue or I'll fills ya full of daylight."*

Make with the ... (idiom) — Quickly provide what was requested. *"Make with the goods or I'll fill you full of lead, see?"*

Malarkey (n) — False or foolish talk; B.S. *"Taffy Brooks tried to hit me up for a loan with the usual bit of malarkey."*

Mamma (n) — Woman. *"The redhead at the bar is one mamma I wouldn't mind tucking me in for the night."*

Map (n) — A person's face. *"With a map like his, Toothless Tommy wasn't going to win any beauty contests."*

Marbles (n) — 1. Brains or wits. *"Have you lost your marbles?"* 2. Pearls or gems. *"With a flourish he produced the marbles from the hotel robbery."*

Mark (n) — Victim (or intended victim) of a con game. *"Rule number one is to make sure your mark isn't packing heat."*

Massage a chin (v) — Hit someone. *"I plan to massage the chin of the next mug who even looks at me sideways."*

Mauler (n) — A set of brass knuckles. *"Maybe if you took that mauler off your hand we can talk like civilized people."*

Mazuma (n) — Money. *"Make with the mazuma you owe me or you'll be wearing a Chicago overcoat."*

Dictionary

Meat (n) — A particular person or new member of a group. *"Why the new meat? I thought our gang was complete."*

Meat wagon (n) — Ambulance. *"After Dizzy Dan introduced his jalopy to a brick wall, the meatwagon carted him away."*

Merchandise (n) — Stolen goods. *"If we don't deliver the merchandise to that fence by noon the deal's off."*

Mesca (n) — Marijuana. *"Solly Meyer said he'd rather get paid in mesca than moolah; I guess he thinks he can resell it and make even more."*

Mexican Divorce (n) — A quickie divorce in Mexico. *"She came back with a Mexican divorce and a stud named Juan."*

Mickey or Mickey Finn (n) — A drink laced with knockout drops. *"I slipped him a mickey finn so he'll be out for hours."*

Midnight auto supply (n) — Car parts obtained by theft. *"It was obvious he'd restored his heap with a collection of parts from the midnight auto supply."*

Mill (n) — Typewriter. *"I poured myself a slug of rot-gut, sat down in front of my mill, and began to put the story down on paper."*

Milquetoast (n) — Timid man. *"Are you going to be a milquetoast or are you going to stand up for yourself?"*

Mind your potatoes (idiom) — Mind your own business. *"Mind your potatoes, snarled Meathook Mahoney when I asked one too many questions."*

Minx (n) — A sassy, calculating, or brashly flirtatious woman. *"That minx sure has a lot of spunk."*

Mish-mash (adj or adv) — All messed up. *"Between the alarm going off, a useless yegg, and cops everywhere, the job turned into a real mish-mash."*

Mitts (n) — Hands. *"Keeps your mitts off my gat."*

Mob (n) — Organized crime syndicate. *"If you cross the mob, you're asking to get rubbed out."*

Moll (n) — Mobster's girlfriend, often a bimbo. *"To be a gun moll, you need to learn to chew gum, walk in high heels, and wear a skirt two sizes too small – all at the same time."*

Moniker (n) — 1. Name, or assumed name. Alias. *"Speedy Nichols proved he wasn't the sharpest knife in the drawer when he chose Slowpoke Dimes as his moniker."*

Monkey stick (n) — Walking cane. *"He struck quite the dandy with his top hat, cutaway coat and monkey stick."*

Mooch (v) — Ask for something without paying for it. *"Why don't you go mooch off somebody else for a change, you bumpkin?"*

Mooch or moocher (n) — Someone who excessively asks for things without offering to pay. *"I'm afraid if I put the touch on my brother for the fifth time this month he might think I'm a mooch."*

Mooncalf (n) — A dimwitted or foolish person. *"I can't believe I got stuck with that mooncalf nephew of Frankie's on such a delicate job."*

Mook (n) — Foolish, contemptible person. *"That mook doesn't know crap from Shinola."*

Moolah (n) — Money. *"Moneybags Mabley has more moolah than he knows what to do with."*

Moonshine (n) — Homemade whiskey. *"Careful that moonshine doesn't make you blind."*

Mouthpiece (n) — Lawyer. *"With a smart mouthpiece I should only serve a nickel."*

Moxie (n) — Guts; confidence; chutzpah. *"It takes a lot of moxie to stand up to Icepick Taylor in front of his gang."*

Mud pipe (n) — Opium pipe. *"On the table was a mud pipe, a couple of half smoked reefers, and an empty bottle of rye. On the floor was Butch."*

Muff (n) — Toupee. *"Poor Jackson was found with three pills in his chest, without benefit of his peepers or his muff."*

Mug (n) — 1. Man (demeaning). *"Which one of you mugs wants to get plugged first?"* 2. A person's face. *"He had a mug made for radio, not the movies."*

Mug (v) — To rob or accost someone. *"Lou Jackson got mugged in an alley on the south side last night."*

Muggle (n) — Marijuana cigarette. *"If you're wondering what happened to the muggles you had hidden in your desk, I donated them to the local fund for underprivileged P.I.s."*

Muscle (n) — Hired thug. *"When Rocco showed up with some hired muscle, I knew I was in for a rough time."*

Mush (n) — A person's face. *"The mush on that guy was the stuff of nightmares."*

N

Nabbed (v) — Caught by the authorities. *"Right after I lifted some mark's wallet I was nabbed by the house dick."*

Nailed (v) — Caught by the authorities. *"Chucky got nailed helping himself to the five-finger discount at the five and dime."*

Naked (n) — Unarmed. *"Upon closer reflection, it was rather careless to go naked to meet a known felon in a dark alley."*

Nance or Nancy (n) — Effeminate man or homosexual. *"You're acting pretty tough for a nance without a gat."*

Nautch house (n) — Bordello. *"I tried to visit that nautch house Trixie works at but they were afraid my mug would frighten the girls."*

Neck stretched (v) — To be hanged. *"Icing a judge sounds like a pretty good way to get your neck stretched."*

Negro (n) — African-American person. *"Meet me at the new nightclub where our negro friend works."*

Nevada gas (n) — Cyanide, especially that used in executions. *"I'd rather take a deep breath of Nevada gas than go out with that chippie again."*

News hawk (n) — Newspaper reporter. *"There was always a news hawk or two hanging around the precinct waiting room."*

Newsie (n) — Street-corner newspaper seller, most often a child. *"Hey, that newsie clipped me out of my change."*

Nibble (n) — Have a drink. *"Hope you don't mind if I have a nibble of your good bourbon."*

Nick (v) — To steal. *"I left my new watch in the gym locker and somebody nicked it."*

Night trap (n) — After-hours nightclub or bar, usually seedy. *"The joint had changed names and owners, but still had the universal frowst of every night trap."*

Nippers (n) — Handcuffs. *"I think my appearing in court in nippers and striped pajamas may have influenced the jury somewhat."*

Nix (v) — Stop doing something, often said with urgency. *"Nix, nix! Here comes the security guard."*

No dice (idiom) — Failure. *"I tried the combination for the safe Donny G. gave me, but no dice."*

No sale (idiom) — Rejection or disbelief. *"You want me to help you rob an armored car? No sale."*

No soap (idiom) — Without success; a negative outcome; a denial of an expectation or request. *"I looked in all the places we used to meet, but alas no soap."*

Noggin (n) — Head. *"Nicky was strolling down the street when a falling brick caught him right in the noggin."*

Noodle (n) — Head or brains. *"Maybe you should use the old noodle a little more before suggesting something stupid."*

Nookie (n) — Sex. *"Jimmie Wilson was snuffed while having a little afternoon nookie with another man's wife."*

Now you're on the trolley! (idiom) — On the right track; now you understand. *"First put on your socks, then your shoes. Now you're on the trolley!"*

Number (n) — Woman. *"Get a gander at that number wearing the pearls and fancy dress."*

Nuts! (intj) — Forceful expression of disdain, disappoint, or disbelief. *"Nuts if I'll come out with my hands up, coppers!"*

Oakie (n) — Someone who fled the dust bowl and parts East during the Great Depression; an unsophisticated, unwelcome itinerant; lit. someone from Oklahoma. *"You don't have to be from Oklahoma to be an Oakie."*

Oday (n) — Money. *"If you've got the oday, I've got the time."*

Ofay (n) — African-American term for white person. *"Man, that brother was so blitzed he thought I was an ofay."*

Off (v) — To murder someone. *"Big Louie would off someone as casually as swatting a fly on a July afternoon."*

Off the track (idiom) — Completely lose it, especially becoming violent. *"When Paulie Pliers hears his best gal left town he'll go completely off the track."*

Oiled (adj) — Inebriated. *"You ought to stay oiled more often; it improves you."*

On a toot (idiom) — On a drinking binge. *"I haven't seen Nick the Nose for a week, I think he's off on a toot."*

On the level (adj) — Legitimate or honest. *"You'd better be on the level with me about that night watchman's schedule."*

On the nut (adj) — Broke. *"I got no chance with that babe, I'm on the nut."*

On the shelf (idiom) — Alone and friendless. *"You rat anyone out and you'll find yourself on the shelf in this town."*

On the up and up (idiom) — Legitimate or honest. *"Vinny's gone legit, he's completely on the up and up now."*

Op (n) — Private detective (from *"Operative"*). *"With his threadbare suit and tired shoes he didn't look like your typical op."*

Orphan paper (n) — Bad checks. *"You keep doling out that orphan paper and you're going to end up back in the hoosegow."*

Ossified (adj) — Inebriated. *"I was totally ossified after an evening swilling bathtub gin."*

Outfit (n) — Criminal gang or enterprise. *"If you want to run with Momo's outfit, you'll have to prove yourself first."*

Oyster fruit (n) — Pearls. *"That sheba had enough oyster fruit on her neck to open her own jewelry store."*

P

Pack heat (adv) — Carry a gun. *"It was always a good idea to pack heat when you went down to the docks after dark."*

Pal (or pally) (n) — Form of address for a man, sometimes affectionate, sometimes disrespectful. *"Listen pally, nobody pushes Eddie McMurphy around, see?"*

Palooka (n) — Man, probably a little stupid or oafish. *"She couldn't help but fall for the next big palooka she ran into. She liked them big and dumb."*

Pan (n) — A person's face. *"Fat Tony didn't look so good after he got smashed in the pan with a two by four."*

Pancake (n) — A woman. *"I wish I had a nice pancake to spend some time with before I go back to the stoney lonesome."*

Pansy (n) — Homosexual or effeminate male. *"Only a pansy would wear a lavender shirt to a dice game."*

Paper flower (n) — A pretty but very delicate, perhaps too delicate, woman. *"She may look dainty but trust me, she's no paper flower."*

Paper sandwich (n) — A book. *"From the looks of him, that goombah had never enjoyed a paper sandwich in his life."*

Paste (v) — Punch. *"Take that back or I'll paste you right in the puss."*

Patsy (n) — Someone who takes the blame for an act they didn't commit. *"What we needed was some palooka to be our patsy for this caper."*

Paw (n) — A person's hand, usually a male. *"He reached out a paw the size of a Christmas ham and helped me off the grimy floor."*

Pea shooter (n) — Gun, specifically a handgun. *"Put that pea shooter away before I take it away and beat you with it."*

Peach (v) — Inform on. *"If you want me to peach on Lefty's outfit you'd best take out some life insurance."*

Peanut grifter (n) — A small-time criminal or operator. *"You're just a peanut grifter in a cheap, traveling circus of a town."*

Peeper (n) — Detective. *"What we don't need right before a big job is some peeper sniffing around because you've been dipping wallets."*

Dictionary

Peepers (n) — Eyes. *"Baby, you've got the most gorgeous peepers I've ever seen."*

Peg (n) — An alcoholic drink. *"Let's go to Joe's; I could use a peg myself."*

Pen (n) — Prison. *"If I get made for this heist, I'll go back to the pen for good."*

Peterman (n) — Safecracker (usually specializing in explosives). *"To get into that vault what we need is a good peterman."*

Petrify (v) — Freeze (as when being held at gunpoint). *"Okay, petrify or you get filled full of holes."*

Piece (n) — Gun, specifically a handgun. *"Nobody touches Pete's piece, ever."*

Piece of the action (n) — A cut or percentage of an illegal activity. *"If you want my help you got to cut me in for a piece of the action, see?"*

Pigeon (v) — To inform upon someone. *"If you want to live to see tomorrow you'd better not pigeon."*

Pigeon (n) — A suspect or person of interest; someone to whom you're referring. *"I spotted your pigeon taking a walk on the boardwalk this morning with some pancake I never saw before."*

Piker (n) — Coward. *"Don't pay any mind to his threats; he's actually a piker."*

Pill (n) — 1. Bullet. *"Pipe down or I'll put a pill in you."* Cigarette. 2. *"Hey buddy, got an extra pill for me?"*

Pinch (v) — To arrest or apprehend. *"John YaYa got pinched by the cops right as he was leaving the scene of the crime."*

Pink or Pinkerton (n) — Private detective, especially one working for the Pinkerton agency. *"That guy's been hanging around all day, I think he might be a pink."*

Pins (n) — A woman's legs. *"A set of pins like hers will get her wherever she wants to go."*

Pipe down (v) — Shut up; be quiet. *"Pipe down in there, I can't hear myself think!"*

Pisher (n) — A brash neophyte. *"No, you can't take my place as bag man, you pisher."*

Pitching woo (n) — Making love (or attempting to). *"I think Tommy's over at Stella's pitching woo."*

Plant (n) — Law enforcement officer or informer put into an illegal organization to gather evidence. *"I shoulda seen that know-it-all pisher was a plant all along, before he ratted us out."*

Dictionary

Put a ring in his nose

Plant (v) — 1. Bury. *"Go plant him in the desert with the cactuses."* 2. Leave evidence at a crime scene to incriminate someone. *"Joey claims that knife was a plant and that he's never been to Big Lou's place."*

Plug (v) — Shoot someone. *"Keep your mitts up or I'll plug you."*

Poke (v) — Punch. *"Oh yeah? Well how'd you like a poke in the puss?"*

Pokey (n) — Jail. *"If you don't have enough dough for bail you'll have to spend the week in the pokey."*

Ponies, The (n) — The horse races. *"If Velda finds out I've been playing the ponies again she's liable to plug me."*

Poop (n) — Information; the low-down. *"What's the poop on that new cookie that's been hanging around with Jessie?"*

Poop sheet (n) — Police file on someone, sometimes called a *"rap sheet."*

Pop (v) — 1. Kill. *"Crazy Mike would just as soon pop you as say hello."* 2. Punch. *"Before he could finish his clever insult, the goon popped him in the beezer."*

Pro skirt (n) — Prostitute. *"You could tell by the way she worked the room she wasn't just a girl on the make, she was a pro skirt after some serious moola."*

Prowler (n) — Marked police car. *"Let me know right away if you see any prowlers show up."*

Pug (n) — Boxer. *"Sweet Lou is managing a new pug he says no one can beat in the ring."*

Pull down the curtain (idiom) — Purposefully leave or disappear without notice, i.e. skip town. *"After Joe got caught skimming from the Outfit, he pulled down the curtains."*

Pump (n) — The heart. *"He got plugged right in the pump and was dead before he was halfway to the cement."*

Pump metal (v) — Shoot. *"Maybe I should stop talking and start pumping metal if you ain't gonna make with the merchandise."*

Punk (n) — Two-bit thug or hoodlum. *"Me scared of you? You're just a two-bit punk from palooka-ville."*

Pup (n) — Child. *"I remember when I was a pup; no, actually, I don't."*

Pushover (n) — Someone easily swayed or intimidated. *"That broad's no pushover, she's a pro skirt."*

Puss (n) — A person's face. *"His mug looks like that because his old lady once smacked him in the puss with an iron skillet."*

Put a ring in his nose (idiom) — Boss someone around. *"No one's going to put a ring in my nose, especially no dame."*

Put his lights out (v) — Kill someone. *"Someone was afraid Willy was going to sing so they put his lights out."*

Put on ice (idiom) — 1. Hold incommunicado. *"We'll put him on ice until after the trial is over."* 2. Kidnap. *"Put her on ice until her old man comes up with the ransom."*

Put the arm on (idiom) — Force or otherwise coerce someone to do something against their will. *"Johnny Sausage used his muscle to put the arm on some local shop owners into signing over their businesses."*

Put the bag on (idiom) — Kidnap. *"Vince says to put the bag on one of Tesso's torpedoes and see if we can get him to spill where the hit's going to be."*

Put the screws to (idiom) — Interrogate harshly. *"John Law put the screws to me, but I didn't squeal."*

Put the touch on (v) — 1. Asked to borrow money. *"I was afraid Pete was going to put the touch on me again, so I made myself scarce."* 2. Blackmailed. *"If we can get those incriminating snaps, we can put the touch on that Fat Cat."*

Q

QT (n) — Keep something secret. *"Let's keep where we hid the loot on the QT for now."*

Quail (n) — 1. Young woman, often underage. *"Before you chase that quail, maybe you should familiarize yourself with the Mann Act."*

Queen (n) — Effeminate or flamboyant homosexual. *"There's nothing sadder than an old queen, Manny told me once."*

Queer (n) — Homosexual. *"What are you, queer for that guy?"*

Queer (v) — To ruin something. *"Keep your mouth shut about the other buyers or you'll queer the deal."*

Quiff (n) — Woman of loose virtue. *"Making it with that quiff is about as hard as falling off a log."*

Quits (n) — 1. Even; debts repaid. *"Here's your half of the take; now we're quits."*

R

Racetrack clothes (n) — Flashy or perhaps gaudy attire (often male). "*He looked so out of place he stuck out like racetrack clothes at a funeral.*"

Rack out or hit the rack (v) — Go to sleep. "*Let's hit the rack, we've got a big day tomorrow.*"

Racket (n) — 1. A dishonest or even illegal scheme. "*Johnny's got some new racket with real estate over on the Eastside.*" 2. Line of work. "*So, bub, what's your racket?*"

Rag (n) — Newspaper. "*You're just some two-bit news hawk looking for an angle your two-bit rag can print.*"

Rag-a-muffin (n) — Dirty child, street kid. "*That rag-a-muffin just stole my wallet!*"

Rags (n) — Clothes. "*Nothing makes a guy feel like a million simoleans like some new rags.*"

Railroad bull (n) — Private security guard hired by the railroads to keep free riders off and guard any freight. "*See you in Cleveland unless the railroad bulls get me.*"

Rap (n) — Criminal conviction. "*Who's going to take the rap for that heist?*"

Rat (n) — Informant. "*Frankie is a lot of things, but he's no rat.*"

Rat (v) — To inform on. "*Whoever rats on Fat Tony is going to end up wearing cement shoes.*"

Rattler (n) — Locomotive train. "*I hopped a rattler to the coast but a railroad bull caught me and gave me the once over.*"

Redbird (n) — Seconal; a barbiturate drug often used as a sleeping pill. "*There were enough redbirds in that sham sawbones's office to put half the city to sleep for a week.*"

Redhot (n) — Cheap hoodlum. "*I'd feel more inclined to believe your benign intentions if you hadn't sent a redhot after me first.*"

Red-light (v) — To throw someone out of a moving vehicle (presumably to their death). "*Drive him over the Triborough and red-light him.*"

Reefer (n) — Marijuana cigarette. *"Don't get caught by the narcs with that reefer in your pocket."*

Revenuer (n) — IRS agent. *"There are no revenuers around here, you bumpkin."*

Rhino (n) — Money. *"Where's the rhino from that train job you pulled?"*

Ringer (n) — 1. A professional posing as an amateur. *"I thought this was a friendly game, but you put in a ringer."* 2. A fake object. *"He swapped the real diamond necklace for a ringer."*

Ritzing (n) — Treat condescendingly. *"I don't mind your ritzing me, but you're wasting your time trying to cross-examine me."*

Rock, The (n) — Alcatraz prison. *"Junkie George liked to hint that he had spent a stretch on The Rock but no one believed him."*

Rocks (n) — Diamonds. *"Those rocks are too hot for me. Try taking them to that uncle on Broadway."*

Roscoe (n) — Gun, specifically a handgun. *"These two punks had me cornered, see? But they didn't know I had a roscoe, see?"*

Rot gut (n) — Cheap booze, usually whiskey or rye. *"That rot gut is cheap, but it'll make you go blind."*

Roundheels (n) — A loose woman. *"I thought Sally was a class act, but the guys told me she was a real roundheels."*

Rub out (v) — To kill. *"Get in the mob's way and they'll rub you out."*

Rube (n) — Unsophisticated or easily duped person; dumb person. *"Don't be such a rube, that's a real work of art."*

Rug (n) — Toupee. *"You're not fooling anyone with that rug on your head, it looks like it needs a good dusting."*

Rumble (the) (n) — The latest news. *"Hey Tony, what's the rumble in your neighborhood?"*

Rummy (n) — An alcoholic or bum. *"He had the rheumy eyes and gin blossoms of a professional rummy."*

Rumpus (n) — Commotion. *"What's all the rumpus about in here?"*

S

Safe cracker (n) — Thief who specializes in opening safes, either by working the combination or using explosives. *"To get to the rocks we're after, we're going to need a first-rate safe cracker."*

Safe ripper (n) — Thief who specializes in opening safes. *"He's such a good safe ripper it's like watching an artist work."*

Sap (n) — 1. A blackjack. *"I saw the sap coming down and then all I saw was stars."* 2. A schmuck. *"Just because I'm in love doesn't mean I'm a sap."*

Sap (v) — To hit with a blackjack, usually knocking one unconscious. *"That copper didn't even say a word, just walked right up and sapped me."*

Savvy (v) — Understand. *"I don't savvy what that guy's talking about."*

Sawbones (n) — Doctor. *"After getting sapped, it's best to visit a sawbones."*

Sawbuck (n) — A ten-dollar bill. *"I'll tell you what you want to know but it'll cost you a sawbuck."*

Scatter (n) — A hideout or place to lay low. *"We need a good scatter until the heat blows over."*

Schlemiel (n) — Bungler, a clumsy or inept person. *"Way to go, sport. You're a real schlemiel."*

Schlep (n) — To haul around. *"Don't expect me to schlep this bag of loot around until we find a nice, quiet scatter."*

Schlimazl (n) — A consistently unlucky person. *"After having coffee spilled on him, getting splashed by a jitney, and then having his wallet lifted, he was beginning to feel like a real schlimazl."*

Schmuck (n) — A person so foolish they're contemptible. *"Don't point that heater at me you schmuck, it's not even loaded!"*

Schnoz (n) — Nose. *"He had a schnoz that looked like a rotted turnip."*

Schtick (n) — Gimmick. *"Benjie's always got some kind of schtick he's running on the tourists."*

Scram (v) — Leave, often quickly. *"We'd better scram before the flatfoots show up."*

Scratch (v) — Kill. *"Take him out to the river tonight and scratch him, boys."*

Scratch (n) — Money. *"I'd like to join you, but I don't have any scratch until payday."*

Scratcher (n) — A forger. *"Find us a good scratcher to make these papers look legit."*

Screw (n) — Guard, usually a jail or prison guard. *"Hey screw, we got a sick man in here."*

Screwy (n) — Irrational or out of place. *"You're acting all screwy. How many muggles did you have today?"*

Second story man (n) — Burglar who prefers to enter from unlocked upstairs windows. *"The best jewel theif is always a second story man."*

Section eight (adj) — Crazy. *"He convinced the shrink he was a real section eight, so he got off easy."*

See? (intj) — Understand. *"I'm no monkey, see? I know a thing or two about a thing or two, see?"*

Send someone's mother flowers (idiom) — Kill someone. *"Careful how you talk to me or I'll be sending someone's mother flowers."*

Send up (v) — To send (or be sent) to prison. *"No way they're ever sending me up again."*

Shake-down (n) — Extortion. *"This isn't a shakedown, it's a business transaction. You get what you need and I get what I want. I'm a legitimate businessman, see?"*

Shamus (n) — Detective, or private detective. *"Looks like you had a shamus shadowing you the whole time you were casing the joint."*

Sharp (n) — A cheater, a swindler – often specializing in schemes using playing cards. *"Never play cards with a sharp like Walter unless you want to get fleeced."*

Sheba (n) — Woman with sex appeal. *"I was about to hit the bricks when this real sheba walked into the bar."*

Sheik (n) — Attractive man. *"They were the best-looking couple at the party, a real sheba and her sheik."*

Shekels (n) — Money. *"One thing Carmine was good at, and that was holding onto his shekels."*

Shill (n) — Accomplice of a swindler or con man who acts as an enthusiastic, anonymous participant in order to entice others. *"What separates the average grifters from the great ones is how good of a shill they have working the crowd."*

Shine (n) — 1. Moonshine. *"Give me a swig of that shine unless you done finished the jug."* 2. Pejorative for a black person. *"Just because you go to Harlem doesn't mean some shine is going to roll you."*

Dictionary

Shiner

Shiner (n) — Black eye. *"I see your old lady imparted you another shiner."*

Shiv (n) — A knife, often a home-made knife in prison. *"Make too many enemies in stir and you're liable to wind up with a shiv in your back."*

Shiv (v) — To knife someone. *"Rocko was in the chow line when someone shivved him right in front of the desserts."*

Shoot your mouth (or face) off (idiom) — To talk out of turn or inappropriately. *"Unless you want a fat lip, don't shoot your mouth off in front of Big Ted."*

Shove off (adv) — Leave the scene. *"We should shove off before the heat comes down on us."*

Shylock (n) — Loan shark. *"A shylock's only as good as the muscle he's got that can go and collect."*

Shyster (n) — An unscrupulous (usually) lawyer. *"That shyster took my cabbage but didn't even show up for my court hearing."*

Silk (adj) — All okay so far. *"You worry too much, everything's silk."*

Simoleans (n) — Money. *"I'd never seen so many simoleans in one place when that butter and egg man opened his safe."*

Sing (v) — Confess; snitch. *"The cops are expecting me to sing, but they got another thing coming."*

Sinker (n) — Donut. *"Give that flatfoot a sinker and cup of joe, that'll keep him busy."*

Sister (n) — Woman. *"Listen sister, if you don't like men making eyes at you then don't go out dressed like a B-Girl."*

Sitting pretty (adv) — In an enviable position. *"Once we get that lettuce Benny the Baker owes us, we'll be sitting pretty."*

Six-shooter (n) — Gun, specifically a revolver. *"I could see the six-shooter he had tucked in his waist."*

Skate (n) — An easy woman. *"She looks like a respectable dame but she's really just a skate."*

Skate around (v) — To be promiscuous referring to a woman. *"Molly can't wait for her old man to leave on business so she can skate around town."*

Skeleton key (n) — A filed-down key used to open many types of locks. Also called a Pass Key. *"Using a skeleton key, he quickly opened the lock and slid into the room's inky darkness."*

Skid row (n) — Run down area inhabited by unsavory types. *"He's such a shmuck he wouldn't know skid row from Beverly Hills."*

Skin flick (n) — Pornographic movie. *"You just don't take a respectable* dame to a skin flick. Well, not on the first date."

Skinny (n) — Information. "*Give me the skinny on that knockout ankle with the amazing pins.*"

Skip (v) — 1. To quickly and surreptitiously leave town. To leave without paying. "*As soon as he gets the chance, you know Robert the Rabbit is going to skip.*"

Skirt (n) — Woman. "*So, what's a nice skirt like you doing in a dump like this?*"

Skivvies (n) — Undergarments. "*The cops rousted Jimmy out of bed and hauled him downtown in only his skivvies.*"

Slant (n) — Viewpoint or angle. "*What's your slant on this whole prohibition rigmarole?*"

Slapper (n) — Prostitute or easy woman. "*That old slapper still has nice bubs.*"

Sleuth (v) — To investigate, often surreptitiously or without official sanction. "*Now that everyone had gone home, it was time to do a little sleuthing to see what I could discover.*"

Sleuth (n) — A private detective. "*What kind of sleuth doesn't carry a magnifying glass?*"

Slip the noose (idiom) — To escape an unfavorable situation, often unexpectedly. "*While the flatfoot was looking the other way I was able to slip the noose and walk right out the front door.*"

Slug (n) — 1. A punch. "*Imagine my surprise when my sweetie greeted me with a slug instead of a kiss.*" 2. A bullet. "*It didn't take a genius to see the hole the slug had made in the door.*" 3. A shot of alcohol. "*What I really wanted was a slug of whisky and a gasper.*"

Slush-pump (n) — Trombone. "*Nobody plays the slush-pump like Tommy Dorsey.*"

Smackers (n) — Money. "*Harry's peepers went wide when he saw all the smackers in the safe.*"

Smart cookie (n) — A clever or wily person. "*You must think you're some smart cookie the way you were able to barber your way out of trouble.*"

Smart-guy (n) — Unfriendly reference to a cocky or self-assured person. "*One more wisecrack, smart-guy, and you'll be wearing a wooden kimono.*"

Smells of the bucket (idiom) — Ex-convict. "*You smell of the bucket; where'd you do time?*"

Smoke (v) — 1. To kill. "*Next time, don't smoke the guy before he tells you where he's stashed the goods.*" 2. Pejorative term for a black person. "*Call Jones a smoke again and he'll rearrange your face free of charge.*"

DICTIONARY

Smoke wagon

Smoke wagon (n) — Gun, specifically a handgun. "*Go ahead, skin that smoke wagon and let's see who walks away from here.*"

Snaps (n) — Photographs. "*Whoever's got those incriminating snaps of the mayor has a lot of juice at city hall right now.*"

Snap a cap (v) — Shoot at someone. "*He turned to snap a cap at me, but I was too fast.*"

Snatch (v) — Kidnap. "*Sam the Sicilian ordered his goons to snatch Eddie before he sang.*"

Sneak (v) — Steal. "*If she got a chance, she'd sneak that necklace and beat it.*"

Sneak (v) — Leave, go away, scram. "*If you're not here to play cards then sneak, buddy.*""

Sneezer (n) — Jail. "*Make sure you don't get tossed in the sneezer by some prowl car boys.*"

Snitch (n) — Informant. "*I'm no snitch; I gots inte-gritty, see?*"

Snitch (v) — To inform on. "*No one ever snitches on the Kosher Nostre and hangs around to spend their ducats.*"

Snooper (n) — Detective. "*Some new snooper from the precinct has been poking his nose around my business all week.*"

Snoot (n) — Nose. "*Asking questions like that is liable to get you a bust in the snoot.*"

Snort (n) — A drink, usually straight. "*Well, maybe just one snort before I hit the road.*"

Snowbird (n) — Cocaine user. "*He had the beady eyes and frosted upper lip of a serious snowbird.*"

Snuffed (v) — Killed, murdered. "*I heard somebody snuffed Nicky Bones and red lighted him on the interboro expressway.*"

Soak (v) — To pawn. "*I'm so flat I had to soak the watch my mom gave me when I graduated Joliet.*"

Soda Jerk (n) — Dinette or soda fountain worker. "*That rube of a soda jerk didn't even know how to make an egg cream.*"

So's your old lady (idiom) — A hostile rejoinder signifying strong disagreement, not recognized for its cleverness. "*I'm stupid? Well, well, so's your old lady.*"

Soldier (n) — Male form of address. "*There's no need to put on the tough guy act, soldier.*"

Soup (n) — 1. Trouble. "*We'll really be in the soup if the cops show up.*"

Dictionary

Squeal

2. Nitroglycerin. *"The last time you tried to blow a safe you dropped the soup and almost went up instead."*

Soup job (n) — Robbery using nitroglycerin to open a door or safe. *"The tumblers on that safe lock are too quiet – this calls for a soup job."*

Souse (n) — An alcoholic. *"A souse like Fat Frank would sell his mother for a snort of rot-gut."*

Soused (v) — Inebriated. *"Being soused on Old Grand-dad at nine in the morning is generally considered bad form."*

Spats (n) — Fancy footwear. *"With a top hat and spats, he must be headed to the Ritz."*

Speakeasy (n) — Secret establishment selling liquor during prohibition. Later, any disreputable drinking establishment. *"The hooch in that new speakeasy is a lot better than the bathtub gin that Joey makes."*

Specs (n) — Eyeglasses. *"Are those specs just for show or do you really have bad peepers?"*

Spend a penny (idiom) — Go to the bathroom. *"I have to go spend a penny; be right back."*

Spifficated (adj) — Inebriated. *"Nick showed up on Stella's doorstep reeking of bourbon and extremely spifficated."*

Spill (v) — To inform on. *"If you spill about the Purple Gang you might get off easy with the judge."*

Spillikin (n) — A fragment or splinter. *"After he was done cleaning up the crime scene no amount of sleuthing would turn up a spillikin of evidence."*

Spinach (n) — Money. *"I've got no spinach to buy any spinach – or anything else to eat."*

Spitting (v) — Talking. *"Chico was famous for spitting all night without actually saying anything."*

Spondulix (n) — Money. *"Fork over the spondulix or you'll be wearing cement shoes at the bottom of the East River."*

Square (adv) — Be honest; to tell the truth. *"I'm being totally square with you."*

Squawk (v) — To complain. *"Quit squawking about the prices, you've got enough spondulix and then some."*

Squawk box (n) — Speakerphone. *"Put Bela on the squawk box so we can all hear him at the same time."*

Squeal (v) — To inform on. *"Rusty would never squeal on the rest of the gang, even if they gave him the third degree."*

Squeeze (n) — 1. Woman or girlfriend. *"Tommy's new squeeze is a real looker."* 2. Extortion or bribe money. *"It took a lot of squeeze to find a doctor who wouldn't ask any questions."*

Squeeze box (n) — Accordion. *"The rest of the band had succumbed to the hooch, but Johnny on the squeeze box played on with only slightly tangled fingers."*

Squibbed (v) — Shot with a firearm. *"I don't take kindly to being squibbed at in my own office."*

Squiffed out (idiom) — Passed out from drunkenness. *"Halfway through my story I realized she wasn't listening intently to my every word, she was just squiffed out on the couch."*

Squirt metal (v) — To shoot at. *"I knock on the door and the next thing you know someone inside starts to squirt metal at me."*

Stake out (v) — To watch surreptitiously; to surveil. *"We need to know the bank manager's routine, so we'll have to stake out the place for a couple of weeks."*

Steamed (v) — Very angry. *"Boy was he steamed when that dame took his dough then pulled down the curtains."*

Step off (v) — To execute by hanging. *"I won't step off just to protect Smitty and the rest of the bunch."*

Stick of T (n) — Marijuana cigarette. *"The sharp odor told me he'd just lit up a stick of T."*

Stick up (n) — Robbery, usually at gun point. *"Everybody grab some air. This is a stick up."*

Stiff (adj) — Inebriated. *"Carmen was so stiff last night she asked Ugly Joe to dance."*

Stiff (n) — Dead body. *"Where are we going to hide this stiff until we can get some quicklime and shovels?"*

Stilts (n) — Woman's legs. *"At first all I saw was a great pair of stilts, but when I looked up they were topped by a sheba I'd never seen before."*

Sting (n) — A con game. *"The perfect sting is one where the mark never even knows he's been conned."*

Stir (n) — Prison. *"If the cops catch me with any hot merchandise, they'll throw me right back in stir."*

Stompers (n) — Boots. *"From my vantage point lying on the ground, I noticed my assailant had a nice pair of stompers I was about to become very familiar with."*

Stonewall (v) — Hold back information or play for time. *"Stonewall the cops while I stash the evidence."*

Dictionary

Syndicate

Stoney lonesome (n) — Prison. *"A man can lose hope inside the walls of the stoney lonesome."*

Stooge (n) — A lackey or obsequious, mindless person. *"A good-looking skirt can turn any guy into a stooge."*

Stool pigeon, or stoolie (n) — Informant. *"Can you believe that gumshoe wanted me to turn stoolie on Frankie the Fox?"*

Strange (n) — Sexual intercourse. *"Gordon had a rule that he'd never pay for strange."*

Stretch (n) — Prison sentence. *"After his third B&E rap, Smitty was headed for a long stretch at Joliet."*

Stringing (v) — Lying or misleading someone, often on multiple occassions. *"Danny the Nose didn't know she'd been stringing him until it was too late."*

Sucker (n) — Someone taken advantage of; a gullible or easily tricked person. *"That Oakie was a real sucker when it came to cards."*

Sucker punch (v) — To hit someone when they aren't expecting it. *"There's no such thing as a fair fight in the Bowery; you distract the guy then sucker punch him."*

Sugar (n) — 1. Money. *"I know you pawned the ice, so where's the sugar?"* 2. Woman. *"Hey sugar, how about a date?"* 3. Affection. *"Gimme some sugar, baby."*

Sugar daddy (n): — Older man who takes care of or gives expensive gifts to a young girlfriend (usually in exchange for sex). *"If she was going to live the lifestyle she wanted, she was going to have to find a new sugar daddy soon."*

Swank or Swanky (adj) — Elegant; upper-class. *"Man, that Ritz is one swank joint."*

Sweetheart (n) — A man or woman. Usually derogatory when referencing a man. *"Yeah, that Sonny is a real sweetheart."*

Swell (n) — A wealthy person. *"One day these swells that look down on us are going to get their comeuppance."*

Swing (v) — Execution by hanging. *"Johnny Jones is going to swing tomorrow at dawn."*

Syndicate (n) — See Mob. *"I told you there is no Syndicate and we'll kill anyone who says otherwise."*

T

T-Man (n) — Government agent, usually working for the Treasury department. *"You can always tell a T-Man by his cheap suit and shiny shoes."*

Tail (v) — Follow. *"Jo-Jo wants you to tail Fingers Morelli and see where he goes in the afternoons."*

Take a powder (idiom) — Leave. *"Take a powder Mikey; Nick and I have to jaw about some private business."*

Take for a ride (idiom) — Drive someone to a secluded spot and kill them. *"Maybe you should take Johnny No Nose for a ride, if you know what I mean."*

Take it on the heel (idiom) — Leave the scene. *"Time for us to take it on the heel before a crowd gathers."*

Take the fall (idiom) — Be punished for something done by another person. *"Alfey says he'll give you 10 large if you take the fall for him."*

Tank (n) — Holding cell in a jail. *"I cooled my heels in the tank while I waited for my mouthpiece to spring me."*

Tank town (n) — A small, unimportant town (used originally to refer to a town at which trains stopped only to take on water.) *"If you've seen one tank town, you've seen them all – and none of them are worth seeing."*

Tart (n) — An easy or trashy woman. *"With her bleached hair, spiked heels and too-short dress she looked like a tart."*

Taxi-dancer (n) — Woman paid by the song to dance with a partner who has bought a dance ticket at a dance hall. *"What kind of sad sack spends his Saturday night with a room of taxi-dancers?"*

Tea (n) — Marijuana. *"You can always pay Bruiser in tea, he loves to smoke the stuff."*

Tell it to Sweeney (idiom) — Dismissive expression of doubt or disbelief. *"Aww, go tell it to Sweeney – I'm not buying your alibi."*

Ten-spot (n) — A ten-dollar bill. *"Ginny put the touch on me for a ten-spot, then went out dancing with some other joe."*

That's the crop (idiom) — That's all there is. *"So we went to the dance and then I took her straight home – that's the crop, I swear."

Thinner (n) — A dime. "*Marv was so flat he didn't have a thinner to his name.*"

Threads (n) — Clothing. "*Mr. Big always wears the best threads you can buy.*"

Three-card monte (n) — See Follow the Lady. "*Lucky Lou could always pick up some cabbage with three-card monte.*"

Throw a Joe (v) — Pass out. "*You don't look so good, are you about to throw a Joe?*"

Throw gloves (v) — Box or fight. "*They settled in to watch the boys throw gloves at one another.*"

Throw lead (v) — Shoot at someone. "*I was standing on the corner minding my own business when this boiler drives by and starts throwing lead.*"

Throwing bones (v) — Playing dice. "*Icepick, Taffy, and Vinny were passing the time out back throwing bones.*"

Ticker (n) — Wristwatch. "*You must be in the chips to have a swell ticker like that.*"

Ticket (n) — A private investigator's license. "*A private eye without a ticket is just another bum looking for work.*"

Tiger Milk (n) — Hard liquor. "*Wine is okay, but Tiger Milk will get the job done quicker.*"

Tighten the screws (idiom) — See *Put the screws to.* "*He sang when Benny 'The Dentist' threatened to tighten the screws.*"

Till (n) — Cash register. "*Let's see how much green there is in the till.*"

Tin (n) — Police badge. "*That tin on his shirt didn't make him very popular in the neighborhood.*"

Tip your mitt (idiom) — Divulge or share what you know. "*Never tip your mitt if you want to keep the upper hand.*"

Trigger man (n) — Person who did the shooting. "*Rumor has it that Skids O'Connell was the trigger man on the Jerry the Weasel hit.*"

Toe-rag (n) — A kid criminal or delinquent. "*A bunch of toe-rags distracted me while one of them pinched my billfold.*"

Tomato (n) — Woman. "*Boy, that gal is one ripe tomato.*"

Tommy gun (n) — A sub-machine gun, short for Thompson sub-machine gun. "*These gunsels drove by in a flivver throwing lead from a tommy gun.*"

Took into chancery (idiom) — To litigate something, or less commonly referring to a hopeless predicament. "*After she plugged her husband, the family fortune went into chancery.*"

Dictionary

Toots (n) — Form of address for a woman (disrespectful). *"Hey toots, how's about you and me have a tumble tonight?"*

Tops (n) — Loaded dice. *"Benny ended up getting smoked when he was caught with some tops while throwing bones with the boys."*

Torch song (n) — Sad song of lost romance. *"That torch song could make the toughest gee mist up like he was chopping a wheelbarrow of onions."*

Torcher (n) — Female singer. *"The new torcher at the Stork Club is really bringing them in."*

Torpedo (n) — Hired thug. *"As a torpedo working for Mr. Big, Bruiser Malloy didn't have to think much."*

Tosspot (n) — An alcoholic. *"That tosspot couldn't remember what he had for breakfast much less what he saw last night."*

Tramp on it (idiom) — Hurry up. *"Someone tripped the alarm, better tramp on it."*

Trap (n) — Mouth. *"I'd shut my trap if I were you, before it catches something disagreeable."*

Trigger man (n) — A hired gunman, usually associated with a contract killing. *"The Feds think Joe Banana was the trigger man on that hit at Frankie's fruit shop."*

Trip for biscuits (idiom) — Wasted effort. *"Well, since the store was already closed that was a trip for biscuits."*

Trollop (n) — A sexually disreputable, easy woman. *"Get out of here and take that trollop with you."*

Tumble (n) — Phone call. *"Give me a tumble at my hotel later."*

Tumble (v) — Sexual intercourse. *"I'll bet that tart will give you a tumble."*

Twist (n) — Woman. *"That twist is on the make for a sugar daddy."*

Two bits (n) — 25 cents. *"For two bits he could get a haircut or a chili dog. Long hair won't hurt you but an empty stomach will."*

Two-bit (adj) — Cheap, shoddy. *"Forget that two-bit shyster and get yourself a real lawyer."*

U

Un-rod (v) — To take away someone's gun. "*How embarrassing to have a 90-pound frail un-rod you in front of the boys.*"

Uncle (n) — Pawn broker. "*Go see that uncle over on Broadway, he's paying out the most.*"

Under glass (adv) — 1. Watched or followed either knowingly or unknowingly. "*I wasn't able to make the meeting. The coppers had me under glass the whole time.*" 2. In jail. "*We don't need to worry about reprisals for a while since the cops have Manny the Mooch under glass.*"

Under your hat (idiom) — To keep something to yourself; to keep information private. "*Let's keep this dope about the location of Chee-Chee's wickiup under our hats for the time being.*"

Underworld (n) — The criminal element, usually referring to groups of organized crime syndicates. "*Gentleman Johnny Genarro was highly placed in the Chicago underworld.*"

Union suit (n) — A one-piece undergarment covering the body and legs, worn by men and boys. "*I'd shed my pyjamas and was reaching for my union suit when there was a knock on the door.*""

Up-town (adj) — Fancy or high-class. "*Thomas was looking very up-town in a white suit and polka-dot shirt.*"

Up-and-down (n) — To look over carefully. "*Am I dreaming or did that Sheba just give me the up and down?*"

V

Vag charge (n) — Vagrancy charge. *"How'd you like to do thirty on a vag charge?"*

Vamoose (v) — To leave. *"I think I hear a siren; we'd better vamoose before the harness bulls show up."*

Vamp (n) — An attractive, seductive woman. *"When discussing vamps, it's hard to not mention Jessica Rabbit."*

Vamp (v) — To act seductively. *"She vamped him like some wicked Jezebel until he was completely under her spell."*

Vig, or Vigorish (n) — Interest on a loan shark's loan. *"You want to borrow and ten large, then the vig is two c-notes a week."*

W

Wage slave (n) — Working class person, someone earning an honest living. *"Being a wage slave is for suckers. I'm gonna be a big cheese in the outfit."*

Wampum (n) — Money. *"Mugsy Monroe didn't have enough wampum to buy his way into the game."*

Warble (v) — To sing, often professionally. *"You got a nice voice. Didn't I hear you warble over at the Alibi Room?"*

Watering hole (n) — Bar. *"If you need me I'll be at my usual watering hole."*

Weak sister (n) — Pushover. *"Stand up for youself and stop being such a weak sister around your girl."*

Wear iron (adv) — Carry a gun. *"I didn't need to frisk this goon to know he was wearing iron."*

Wet blanket (n) — Someone who doesn't want to join in the fun or other activities. *"Join the party and stop being such a wet blanket."*

Wet the beak (v) — 1. To skim money. *"What, I can't wet my beak in this scam?"* 2. Have a drink. *"I'm going to go wet my beak at Carlo's."*

What gives? (idiom) — What do you mean? What's really going on? *"So if you're supposed to be under glass but you're here, what gives?"*

What's eating you? (idiom) — What's the matter? *"No need to bite my head off. What's eating you, anyway?"*

Wheats (n) — Pancakes. *"What I really wanted for breakfast was to wet my beak, not a stack of wheats and some weak java."*

Wheels (n) — Automobile. *"Some of those swells are so loaded they get a new set of wheels twice a year."*

Whistlin' Dixie (n) — Wasting time, speaking idly. *"When I say I'm about to score really big, I'm not just whistling Dixie."*

White (n) — Gin. *"Sidney, set me up with a tall glass of white – neat."*

Whoopee (n) — Sexual intercourse. *"He's washin' dishes and baby clothes, he's so ambitious he even sews, that's what you get for makin' whoopee."*

Dictionary

Widget

Widget (n) — Thing, gadget. *"What's that widget you keep fooling with?"*

Wikiup (n) — Home. *"I think Sammy went back to his wikiup to sleep it off."*

Wire (n) — A telephone. *"Get me Frankie the Thumb on the wire, post-haste!"*

Wisacre (n) — Smart-aleck. *"Keep being a wiseacre and see what that gets you when Rocko shows up."*

Wisenheimer (n) — A joker, usually used pejoratively. *"Some wisenheimer at headquarters nicknamed him Sparky after he was almost electrocuted."*

Wolf (n) — One who chases the ladies, a ladies' man. *"He's a real wolf with the ladies unless his wife's around, then he's a mewling puppy."*

Wooden kimono (n) — Coffin. *"Try that again and you'll get fitted for a wooden kimono."*

Woodpile (n) — Xylophone. *"When he finished his solo on the woodpile the crowd went wild."*

Woolies (n) — Undergarments. *"When they found the body, all he was wearing were his woolies and a grin."*

Wop (n) — Pejorative term for a person of Italian descent. *"If you want to know about anything happening in Flatbush, go ask that wop with the vegetable cart near Prospect."*

Worker (n) — Woman who tricks or uses men for money or gain. *"Stay away from that vamp, she's a real worker."*

Wren (n) — Woman. *"Now that's one high-class wren at that table."*

Wrong gee (n) — The wrong guy, or a mistaken identity. *"That dragnet pulled in a lot of joes, but they were all the wrong gee."*

Wrong number (n) — 1. A mistake; bad information *"You got the wrong number, I was never near Studsy's last night."* 2. Not a good person. *"Stay away from that wrong number, he'll only cause you trouble."*

Y

Yabos (n) — A woman's breasts. *"Stop thinking about her yabos and get your head in the game!"*

Yap (n) — Mouth. *"Shut your yap if you know what's good for you."*

Yard (n) — One hundred dollars. *"I owe that shylock a yard every week just for the vig."*

Yardbird (n) — Someone in prison or who has been in prison. *"I can tell a yardbird a mile off."*

Yegg (n) — 1. Safecracker, sometimes one who's not very skilled, or can only open easy-to-crack locks. *"We don't need an expert for this job, any yegg will do."* 2. Thug. *"I don't know why you keep treating that guy like a yegg when he's respectable."*

Yellow (adj) — Cowardly. *"I ain't yellow, see? I'm just, what do they call it, now ... soi-cumspect, that's it."*

Yellow jacket (n) — Nembutal, a barbiturate once commonly prescribed as a sleeping pill. Known to be highly addictive. *"If you get hooked on yellow jackets, that shyster sawbones will have you in his pocket forever."*

Yentz (v) — To betray or cause harm to occur. *"Tell them how you yentzed Big Joe out of fifty large on that last grift."*

Yid (n) — Pejorative term for a Jewish person. *"Give that Yid half a chance and he'll yentz you any way he can."*

Yodeler (n) — Effeminate man or homosexual. *"Little did he know only yodelers went to that nightclub."*

Yokel (n) — A foolish or unsophisticated provincial person. *"You'd have to be a real yokel to think you can win at three card monte."*

Yutz (n) — Dummy or stupid person. *"You're a real yutz, you know that?"*

Z

Zaftig (adj) — Plump, luscious, desirable. Usually in reference to part of a woman's anatomy. *"That zaftig little minx is curvy in all the right places."*

Zebra (n) — Convicted felon or prisoner wearing a striped prison uniform. *"I'll go down shooting before I become a zebra again."*

Zotzed (v) — Killed, murdered. *"Chinless Joe got zotzed for juicing Big Sal too much."*

Zozzled (adj) — Inebriated. *"After the stag party, Morty was too zozzled to drive."*

Thesaurus

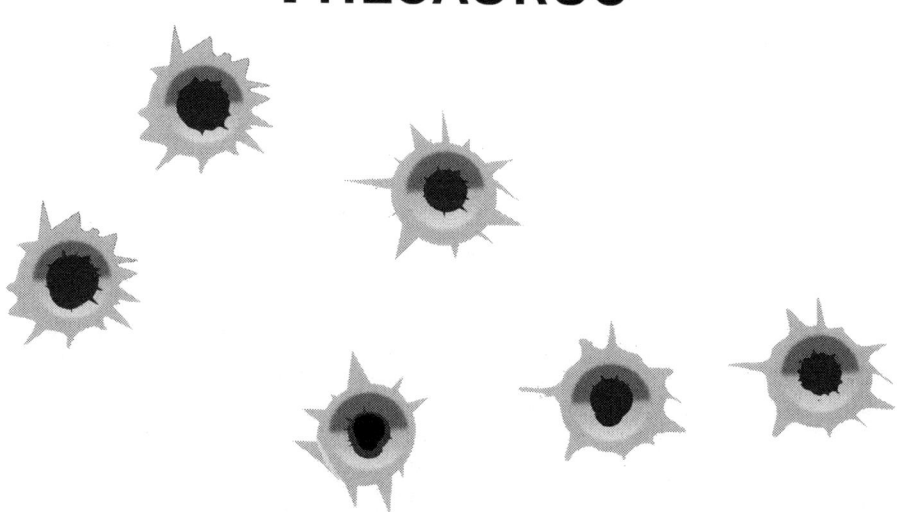

Thesaurus

Alcoholic

Alcoholic/drunkard (n), barfly, bibber, boozehound, gin-fly, lush, rummy, sot, souse, sponge, swill, tosspot, wino.

Alcoholic drink (n), bumper, clam juice, hooch, nightcap, nip, peg, shine, slug, snort, spot, swill, toot, swillbooze.

Armed (adj), heeled, loaded, packing heat.

Bar (n), barrelhouse, clip joint, dive, gin joint, gin mill, juice joint, shebeen, speakeasy, watering hole

Bordello (n), can house, cat house, joy house, house of ill repute, nautch house.

Borrow from (v), cadge, chisel, put the bite on, put the touch on, scrounge, sponge.

Breasts – woman's (n), bazooms, bubs, knockers, yabos.

Cab (n), see Taxi

Call on the phone (v), buzz, drop a nickel, flag, get on the blower, get on the horn, give a tinkle, tumble.

Carrying a gun (adj), see Armed

Child (n), kid, newsie, punk, pup, rag-a-muffin, toe-rag.

Confess or inform on (v), canary, finger, fink, flip, peach, rat out, sing, snitch, spill, squeal, stoolie.

Corpse (n), carcass, dear departed, goner, mortal coil, stiff.

Death (n), the big one, the big sleep, dirt nap, pushing up daisies

Die (v), buy the farm, croak, give up the ghost, kick off

Doctor (n), doc, croaker, leech, quack, sawbones, white coat.

Drugs (n),

Easy woman (n), B-girl, bim, bimbo, chippie, floozy, quaff, roundheels, skate, slapper, tart, taxi-dancer, trollop.

Face (n), map, mug, mush, pan, puss.

Fence (n), front man, lumberer, moving man, receiver.

Gun (n), artillery, bean shooter, canon, chopper (machine gun), gat, hardware, heater, iron, mahaska, ordinance, pea shooter, piece, rod, roscoe, tommy gun.

Handcuffs (n), bracelets, cuffs, darbies, irons, nippers.

Hands (man's, n), dukes, meathooks, mitts, paws.

Hat (n), bucket, chapeau, headgear, lid, topper, fedora.

Inebriated (adj), bent, blotto, boiled, crocked, dead-drunk, half-under, iced to the eyebrows, loaded, lubed, oiled, on a blind, one over the eight, ossified, pickled, plowed, shellacked, smashed, soused, spifficated, squiffed, stiff, tight, zozzled.

Informant (n), finger man, peach, rat, squealer, stoolie, stool pigeon

Interest (as on a loan, n), juice, vig, vigorish.

Jail (n), can, clink, cooler, icebox, lockup, pokey, sneezer, tank. See also *Prison*

Kidnap (v), put on ice, put the bag on, snatch

Kill (v), blip off, bop, bump off burn, chill, clip, croak, erase, hit, knock off, off, pop, punch his ticket, rub out, scratch, smoke, snuff, take for a ride, zotz.

Legs – woman's (n), gams, pins, sticks, stilts.

Loan shark (n), money lender, money-monger, shylock.

Man (n), ape, baby grand (big guy), boy-o, chum, fella, guy, joe, lug, monkey, mug, pal, palooka, soldier, sweetheart.

Money (n), brass, cabbage, cush, dinero, dough, ducats, fiver, geetus, green, jack, lettuce, loot, mazuma, moolah, oday, rhino, sawbuck, scratch, shekels, simoleans, smackers, spinach, spondulix, sugar, thinner, wampum.

Morgue (n), bone house, cold storage, deep freeze.

Nose (n), beak, beezer, button, schnoz.

Old person (n), corpse, Male: Geezer, methuselah, gaffer. Female: crone, hag.

Pawn broker (n), hocker, shylock, uncle.

Playboy (n), cake eater, gigolo, good time Charlie, lech, lothario, pretty boy, skirt chaser.

Thesaurus

Playing dice (v), rolling bones, shooting craps.

Police (n), bluecoat, bull, button, cop, copper, flatfoot, harness bull, heat, John Law, Lizzie Lice (cops in cars).

Prison (n), big house, bucket, caboose, can, cooler, hoosegow, joint, jug, pen, stir, the Castle (Sing-Sing), the Rock (Alcatraz).

Prostitute (n), bat, call girl, doxy, girl of the night, joy girl, lady of the evening, Lousy Liz, pro, pro skirt, working girl.

Punch or hit (n), biff, crown, deck, knuckle sandwich, haymaker, kiss, lick, massage a chin, paste, play chin music, poke, pop, slug, throw gloves.

Restaurant (n), chophouse, greasy spoon, hash house, hot dog stand, roadhouse.

Robbery (n), caper, heist, hold up, job, stick up.

Shoot (v), blast, drill, fill full of daylight, fog, give it to, plug, pump metal, smoke, squib, squirt metal, throw lead.

Speakeasy (n), blind pig, drum, gin mill, juice joint.

Taxi (n), cab, hack, jitney.

Telephone (n), ameche, blower, buzz, horn, wire.

Thug (n), bruiser, enforcer, goon, gorilla, gun-holder, gunpoke, gunsel, hesiter, hitman, hood, loogan, muscle, punk, redhot, soldier, torpedo, trigger man, wrong gee.

Woman (n), ankle, badger, bearcat, bim, bimbo, bird, broad, chickie, chippie, cookie, crone, dame, dish, doll, floozy, frail, girlie, jane, judy, kitten, looker, mama, number, pancake, paper flower, quail, sheba, sister, skirt, tomato, twist, vamp, wren.

Appendix One
The Dozens

12 Noteworthy Noir Novels

12 Trendsetting Gumshoes

12 Hard-Boiled Ink Slingers

12 Noteworthy Noir Novels

Presented below in order of publication are a dozen novels which set the pace for the hard-boiled yarn. You'll probably recognize some of the usual suspects, but hopefully there are a few here which will expand your horizons. If you've seen some of the film adaptations that's great, but the enduring allure of this genre is its wonderful use of language, so pick up a copy, prop your feet up and lose yourself in the shadowy worlds of these tales.

Snarl of the Beast by Carroll John Daly, 1927. This gritty tale set the tone for all hard-boiled P.I. novels to follow, with a ripping first-person narrative, taut writing, a loner protagonist, fallen dames, mysterious clients, and plenty of bodies. In fact, it features one of the first, if not the first, appearance of the term "hard-boiled." Protagonist Race Williams is a hard-charging, take no prisoners private dick with a marked lack of inhibition to employ violence. Mickey Spillane's writing is often compared to Daly's spare, often staccato prose. With this book Daly had perfected the dark, evocative imagery in his writing that would define the genre:

> *"The tin pan notes of a piano drift faintly into the night. A man curses and a window slams. Far distant an ash can clatters on stone and the almost human screech of a cat pierces."*
> Race Williams in *The Snarl of the Beast*.

Red Harvest by Dashiell Hammett, 1929. The never-named Continental Op travels to "Poisonville" where his client is murdered before he arrives. Never one to waste a trip, The Op still secures a contract to clean up the town for his employer, the Continental Detective Agency. It turns out the client had hired some underworld gangs to break a strike, and they never left. Red Harvest is fast-paced, bare-knuckle prose with a high body count. A seminal event in hard-boiled detective literature.

> *"If I don't get away soon I'll be going blood simple like the natives."*
> The Continental Op in *Red Harvest*.

The Maltese Falcon by Dashiell Hammett, 1930. More intricately plotted than most hard-boiled stories up to this time, The Maltese Falcon introduced us to morally ambiguous private eye Sam Spade. Spade was arguably a more richly drawn, less arrogant literary progeny of Race Williams. The novel has all the earmarks of a classic hard-boiled detective story: the solitary private eye, the femme fatale, an oppressive, atmospheric setting, gunsels, and a plot with plenty of twists and turns. The titular Maltese Falcon also popularized the "dingus" or "MacGuffin" in detective fiction, the often arbitrary contrivance which serves as a driver for the plot. Other examples of a MacGuffin include the "letters of transit" in *Casablanca*, a missing person such as "The Thin Man" in *The Thin Man*, "Rosebud" in *Citizen Kane*, or the briefcase in *Pulp Fiction*.

> "You're good. You're very good. It's chiefly your eyes, I think, and that throb you get into your voice when you say things like 'Be generous, Mr. Spade."
> Sam Spade in The Maltese Falcon.

The Thin Man by Dashiell Hammett, 1934. A truly novel novel in the genre. Retired police detective and former Pinkerton, Nick Charles is smart, tough, confident, sometimes self-effacing, and possesses a wicked wit. Charles retired from the detective's bureau after marrying into money and is unashamed and unapologetic about it. His wife Nora is his equal in wit and style. Despite his comfortable retirement, Nick (and Nora) get drawn into a murder mystery. With The Thin Man, Hammett created a unique husband and wife detective duo that has yet to be equaled. Full of playful banter, the novel is less hard-boiled than works featuring Hammett's other detectives (The Continental Op and Sam Spade) and almost reads like a comedy of manners:

> *Nora said: "She's pretty."*
> *"If you like them like that."*
> *She grinned at me. "You got types?"*
> *"Only you, darling – lanky brunettes with wicked jaws."*
> Nick and Nora Charles in The Thin Man.

Build My Gallows High, by Geoffrey Homes, 1946. This classic noir story was made into the classic (but altered) 1947 film noir "Out of the Past," which was remade (even more altered) in 1984 as "Against All Odds." Both great movies, but for a real dose of darkness go to the source. As owner of a small garage in small town California, Red Bailey is trying to escape his messy past as a private detective in New York when he's drawn back into a 10-year-old case that went very, very bad. Murder, betrayal, and a truly nasty femme fatale. You'll keep turning the pages to see if Red can escape his past once and for all.

> *"It would be all right, he kept telling himself, because he wanted it*

to be, because he didn't want to lose her, because he wanted to stay blind. When you create something, you hate to see it dissolve into nothingness."

Red Bailey in *Build My Gallows High*.

The Moving Target, by Kenneth Millar (writing as Ross Macdonald), 1949. Set in Southern California, as so many hard-boiled stories are, this book introduced readers to P.I. Lew Archer. Like Marlowe, Archer was a more nuanced character than many earlier gumshoes. However, if Marlowe's character was introspective, Archer was more outwardly focused on the figures around him. In The Moving Target, Archer's wealthy client is eccentric, to say the least, but begins to pale in comparison to the oddballs Archer runs up against as he searches for her missing husband. As is often the case, things are not what they first appear. The Moving Target also touched on social criticism (also evident in Raymond Chandler's later work), shining a harsh light on the foibles of the rich, the exploitation of the poor and middle class, and the corruption underneath Southern California's shiny façade.

...(my) face had seen too many bars, too many rundown hotels and crummy love nests, too many courtrooms and prisons, post-mortems and police lineups, too many nerve ends showing like tortured worms. If I found the face on a stranger, I wouldn't trust it.

Lew Archer in *The Moving Target*.

One Lonely Night, by Mickey Spillane, 1951. Spillane's Mike Hammer is the archetype of the straightforward, uncomplicated, brutal, and merciless private eye. *One Lonely Night* is one of the better examples of the Hammer novels to explore the character, his motivations, and ruminations on how he fills a necessary place between the law of the courts and the law of the streets. This thankless role only brings Hammer grief and disdain from all sides of the justice system. Still, Hammer has a code and he sticks with it. *One Lonely Night* features the requisite body count, first-person narrative, dangerous women, and pitiless justice which earned Hammer his place in the P.I. pantheon. Communists and corruption don't stand a chance when Hammer turns his attention to them.

"Her body was a milky flow of curves under the translucent gown and when she moved the static current of flesh against sheer cloth made it cling to her in a way that made me hold my breath to fight against the temptation."

Mike Hammer in *One Lonely Night*.

The Long Goodbye, by Raymond Chandler, 1953. Philip Marlowe returns in what Chandler referred to as his best novel. In *The Long Goodbye*, Chandler isn't afraid to shine a not-so-subtle unflattering light on himself as Marlowe is hired to babysit an alcoholic, hack writer trying to finish his latest work. Chandler also makes no bones about using the book for some pointed social commentary regarding the disenfranchisement of the common man by the wealthy and the press/justice system/big business complex. However, Chandler being Chandler, none of this stands in the way of an absorbing and satisfying read.

> *"...I mixed a stiff one and stood by the open window in the living room and sipped it and listened to the groundswell of traffic on Laurel Canyon Boulevard and looked at the glare of the big angry city hanging over the shoulder of the hills through which the boulevard had been cut. Far off the banshee wail of police or fire sirens rose and fell."*
> Philip Marlowe in The Long Goodbye

How Like an Angel, by Margaret Millar, 1962. Meet Joe Quinn, the most down on his luck P.I. you're likely to encounter. Joe has a serious gambling problem. As the story opens, his gambling has relieved of his savings, his girl, his job, even his clothes. Hitching his way, Joe's dumped by a driver at a compound of religious fanatics. There he's asked to locate a man for one of the habitués. Joe takes the job – what else does he have going on? When the subject of his search turns up dead things begin to get complicated. *How Like an Angel* is one of the best examples of Margaret Millar's work in the genre. More than any other writer listed here, Millar's novels are deep dives into the psychological as well as the material world. One of her trademarks is a big twist at the end which only makes you want to read the book again, and *How Like an Angel* is no exception. Point of interest: Margaret Millar was the wife of fellow genre writer Kenneth Millar, who wrote as Ross Macdonald.

> *He'd been in jams before but they'd always involved people, friends to confide in, strangers to persuade. He prided himself on being a glib talker. Now it no longer mattered, there wasn't anyone around to listen.*
> Joe Quinn in *How Like an Angel*.

Devil in a Blue Dress, Walter Mosely, 1990. Fate steps in to lead Ezekiel (Easy) Rawlins into the life of a private detective in this stark, realistic novel set in late 1940s Los Angeles. As an African-American, Easy is uniquely qualified for investigations when they intersect with the black community, an area where white investigators and the police aren't welcome or trusted. Recently laid off from his manufacturing job, a mysterious man offers Easy some easy money to locate a missing woman. Mosely takes us into the underbelly of Los Angeles, exploring race, class and privilege all while spinning a gripping detective story.

> "That girl is the devil. She got evil in every pocket."
> Easy Rawlins in *Devil in a Blue Dress*.

L.A. Confidential, by James Ellroy, 1990. Set in 1950s Los Angeles, one of the best pieces of gritty detective fiction ever put to paper. As the plot peels back like a rotten onion, layers of graft, racism, vice, corruption, and general unseemliness unfold like a wilted flower shedding its petals. There's a very blurry line between good and bad in the novel, as it follows a huge cast of characters including an ambitious police lieutenant, a high-class pimp, call girls surgically altered to resemble movie stars, lowlife reporters, and police thugs. The good are bad, the bad are good, but it all depends on where you stand. Ellroy tells this tale in such a descriptive, absorbing way that you forget you're reading a novel.

> "Some men get the world, some men get ex-hookers and a trip to Arizona. You're in with the former, but my God I don't envy the blood on your conscience."
> Lynn Bracken to Ed Exley in *L.A. Confidential*.

Sin City, Vol. 4, That Yellow Bastard, by Frank Miller, 2004. Miller blends the hard-boiled, noir literary tradition with the graphic novel format, proving that a good story well told works anywhere. The *Sin City* series follows a group of society's outcasts, from a burned-out detective to psychopathic politicians, pedophiles, prostitutes, and a knight-errant goon as they violently intersect. The sparse, crisp dialogue and grim plot mesh perfectly with the stark, minimalist artwork.

> "An old man dies, a little girl lives. Fair trade."
> Detective John Hartigan in *Sin City*.

12 Trendsetting Gumshoes

Following are some fictional characters who have shaped our conception of the hard-bitten Private Eye. The list is heavy on earlier figures, with a few notable exceptions. I hope you'll recognize some old friends and maybe acquaint yourself with a few new ones. The list includes the the writer, the P.I., when they made their first appearance, and a pithy quote that provides some insight into their character.

Lew Archer is a private dick working in Southern California. Created by Ross Macdonald in 1949, Archer's career spanned three decades and 18 full-length novels. Like most of our beloved shamuses (shami?), he was often depressed and alone. Disillusioned with the graft he saw, he left the police department to set up his own detective business. Archer could be more thoughtful than his counterparts and his cases didn't always end tidily. The Archer books are noted for a more sophisticated and literary plotting and style. Word has it Eudora Welty was a big fan so, you know, 'nuff said.

"It was a Friday night. I was tooling home from the Mexican border in a light blue convertible and a dark blue mood."
Lew Archer in *Gone Girl*.

Charlie Chan. Though now somewhat controversial, Chan was created in 1919 by Earl Biggers as a counterpoint to the "Yellow Peril" stereotypes of fiction like Fu-Manchu. Charlie Chan novels often dealt with issues of race, unusual for the time. Chan was low-key and methodical, with a dry wit and dedication to justice. He holds the record in this list for most movie appearances at somewhere north of 50. How can you not like a man who tells his eldest son, who's clad in some flamboyant nightclothes, to be quiet, observing:

"Please. Pajamas loud enough without you making extra noise."
Charlie Chan in *The Jade Mask*.

Nick Charles. Sarcastic, urbane Nick Charles and his wife and partner in crime-solving Nora debuted in Dashiell Hammett's "The Thin Man" in 1934. Charles was an alcohol-marinated witty ex-cop and ex-Pink who retired after marrying a woman of means. Yet somehow retirement didn't stop the couple from getting mixed up in murder and mayhem. Unlike Hammett's other tough-guy creations, Charles struck more of a lighter note and engaged in more witty banter. And while there were times when a harder interior shone through, nobody could banter better than Nick Charles:

> "I said: 'All right, talk, but do you mind putting the gun away? My wife doesn't care, but I'm pregnant.'"
>
> Nick Charles in *The Thin Man*.

The Continental Op was the original "man with no name." Literally. Introduced by Dashiell Hammett in 1927, "The Op's" tales are told in first-person through dozens of stories and novels without ever revealing his true name. The moniker derives from his job with the Continental Detective Agency (a thinly disguised Pinkerton's, for whom Hammett worked for several years.)

Unprepossessing, The Op is not a daredevil. He solves cases because he's diligent, thorough, and persistent, wearing out shoe leather knocking on doors for information. Detecting is a job to him, and he's committed to doing the best he can. He considers himself "the hired man" who's there to get a job done, whether that be flipping burgers or flushing out murderers it was all the same to him. Influences of The Op's methodical style can be seen in Tony Hillerman's Navajo detectives Joe Leaphorn and Jim Chee. He may be balding and portly, but there's no soft, chewy center to The Op. To him violence is simply a tool of the trade, like a wrench to a mechanic:

> "His belly was flabby, and it got softer every time I hit it. I hit it often."
>
> The Op in *Death on Pine Street*.

Phryne Fisher. Glamorous and glib, the fabulous Miss Fisher is the creation of Australian author Kerry Greenwood, debuting in 1989. Even against the milieu of the roaring twenties, she was a handful. Accomplished pilot, driver of her own automobile (!), and skilled in self-defense, she wasn't shy about employing the pearl-handled gold pistol she usually packed. Not content to lead a life pursuing aimless pleasures, she used her wiles and incisive deductive talents to solve cases. While she falls more into the "cozy mystery" genre, you shouldn't get in her way:

> "I gave chase, and he took a shot at me, so I did the only thing I could in the circumstances.... I stabbed him in the shoulder."
>
> Phryne Fisher in *Raisins and Almonds*.

Peter Gunn made his entrance on the small screen in 1958 courtesy of Blake Edwards. To quote from the website thrillingdetective.com, "Suave, sophisticated, hep to the jive, groovin' to the oh-so-cool jazz-bo beat, Peter Gunn was ... a new kind of eye. While other dicks hung out in rundown offices, swilling rotgut, living hand to mouth, loners till the end, cloaked in rumpled trench coats and angst, Gunn hung out at Mother's, a swank jazz club, wearing his Ivy League finest, pitching woo at his best gal, singer Edie Hart, drinking nothing more than an occasional tasteful martini." The Peter Gunn theme by Henri Mancini still rocks to this day with covers from the likes of Aerosmith, Art of Noise, the Blues Brothers, Jeff Beck, the Cramps, Duane Eddy, Dave Grusin, Emerson, Lake & Palmer, Poison Ivy, and countless others.

> "We grow up and we die. Worrying about it just gets us there a little sooner."
>
> Peter Gunn in *The Kill*.

Mike Hammer first showed up in Mickey Spillane's 1947 "I, the Jury." Hammer epitomized the anti-hero. A simple man with simple ways who was dedicated to the truth, Hammer had no qualms about putting down a violent criminal with his beloved .45 Colt. Fearless to a fault, Hammer would walk right into a den of bad guys. There are echoes of the hard-boiled Race Williams in Hammer's no-nonsense, violent approach to his work. Bottom line: Hammer is a hard case and you don't want to be on his bad side.

> "...I was a licensed investigator who knocked off somebody who needed knocking off bad and he couldn't get to me. So I was a murderer by definition and all the law could do was shake its finger."
>
> Mike Hammer in *One Lonely Night*.

Sherlock Holmes, introduced by Sir Arthur Conan Doyle in 1887 as the world's first "Consulting Detective." Holmes was no armchair detective and not afraid to smash someone in the beezer if needed. His combat skills include sword, cane, boxing, and martial arts. Like any proper P.I., Holmes often clashed with the police, was frequently impatient, surly, and a definite loner (aside from his friendship with Watson.) Holmes was comfortable in the seamier sides of London, from opium dens to the alleys of White Chapel. When you get right down to it, Holmes had a lot in common with his literary successors:

> "I think that there are certain crimes which the law cannot touch, and

which therefore, to some extent, justify private revenge."
    Sherlock Holmes in *The Adventure of Charles Augustus Milverton.*

Philip Marlow first appeared in 1939 in "The Big Sleep" by Raymond Chandler. This tough P.I. is big (6'1") unmarried (like most PIs, it seems), and stands out for his character's inner complexity and wry sense of humor. Marlow plays chess (often with himself), enjoys poetry, smokes (Camels), and likes a stiff drink. Despite his gritty profession, Marlow is a man of integrity and wit.

> *"I needed a drink. I needed a lot of life insurance. I needed a vacation. What I had was a coat, a hat and a gun."*
>   Philip Marlowe in *Farewell My Lovely.*

Ezekiel (Easy) Rollins is a tough, smart P.I. first introduced to us by Walter Mosley in his 1990 novel "Devil in a Blue Dress." Easy's tale begins in 1940s Los Angeles, where he falls into being a detective after being laid off from his assembly line job. Easy presents the genre through the lens of an African-American who just wants to care for his modest home and make a living. His wits, tenacity and street sense help him solve his cases, even without benefit of formal police training or a P.I. ticket. Easy is a realist who's fiercely loyal to his friends, even when they happen to be psychopathic killers (I'm looking at you, Mouse.)

> *"A man once told me that you step out of your door in the morning, and you are already in trouble. The only question is, are you on top of that trouble or not?"*
>   Easy Rawlins in *Devil in a Blue Dress.*

Sam Spade, a "hard and shifty fellow" burst onto the scene in Dashiell Hammett's "The Maltese Falcon" in 1929. As a P.I., he was in business with Miles Archer. As a man, he was in bed with Archer's wife. Cynical, fierce (*"When I slap you, you'll take it and like it."*) and morally ambiguous. After his partner is bumped off, Spade wastes no time in removing Archer's name from the office door. Nevertheless, Sam Spade has his own moral compass:

> *"When a man's partner is killed he's supposed to do something about it. It doesn't matter what you thought of him. He was your partner and you're supposed to do something about it."*
>   Sam Spade in *The Maltese Falcon.*

Race Williams sprung from the mind of Carroll John Daly in 1923, years ahead of the Continental Op, Sam Spade and Philip Marlow. Bold and supremely self-confident, P.I. Race Williams is a straight shooter in both senses. He's known in crime circles and law enforcement as someone who always keeps his word and never makes an idle threat. Like most good gumshoes, he lived by his own moral compass which didn't always jibe with society's: "My ethics are my own."

A template for many gumshoes to come, Williams was cynical, pragmatic, and employed violence and gunplay as a matter of course. His reputation as someone who'd just a soon shoot you in the spine as not often negated the need for the actual rough stuff. Many trace a line, and it's a fair comparison, from Race Williams to Mickey Spillane's Mike Hammer as the inheritor of the mantle of the lone, hardheaded, and gritty private detective.

> *"When I wanted a man, I stuck a gun in each pocket and went after him. I'll stand on my legs and shoot it out with any gun in the city. Any time. Any place."*
>
> Race Williams in *The Snarl of the Beast*.

12 Hard-Boiled Ink Slingers

Without good writers there would be no good stories. Below are some mill jockeys who've had an outsized influence on the way we think of crooks and cops, and the lingo we associate with them. These talented writers created their own gritty realities, each adding their own color to the ever-increasing hard-boiled vernacular.

W.R. Burnett (November 25, 1899—April 25, 1982)
Notable Novels/Characters:
Little Caesar (1929), Little Caesar/Rico
The Asphalt Jungle (1949) Dix Handley, Alonzo D. Emmerich

James M. Cain (July 1, 1892—October 27, 1977)
Notable Novels/Characters:
The Postman Always Rings Twice (1934), Frank Chambers
Mildred Pierce (1941), Mildred Pierce
Double Indemnity (1936), Phyllis Nirdlinger

Raymond Chandler (July 23, 1888—March 26, 1959)
Notable Novels/Characters:
The Big Sleep (1939) Carmen Sternwood, *The High Window (1942)* Leslie Murdock, *The Long Goodbye (1953)* Terry Lennox,
all featuring private detective Philip Marlowe

Carroll John Daly (September 14, 1889—January 16, 1958)
Notable Novels/Characters:
The Adventures of Race Williams (Collected stories—1989),
Race Williams
The Complete Cases of Vee Brown, Volume 1 (2014), Vivian "Vee" Brown

Dashiell Hammett (May 27, 1894—January 10, 1961)
Notable Novels/Characters:
The Dain Curse (1928), The Continental Op
The Maltese Falcon (1930), Sam Spade, Brigid O'Shaughnessy
The Glass Key (1931), Ned Beaumont
The Thin Man (1934), Nick Charles, Nora Charles

Chester Himes (July 29, 1909—November 12, 1984)
Notable Novels/Characters
The Real Cool Killers (1959), *Blind Man with a Pistol (1969)*,
"Grave Digger" Jones, "Coffin" Ed Johnson

Elmore Leonard (October 11, 1925—August 20, 2013)
Notable Novels/Characters
Get Shorty (1990), Chili Palmer
Tishomingo Blues (2002), Dennis Lenahan
Road Dogs (2009), Jack Foley, Cundo Rey, Dawn Navarro

Kenneth Millar (as Ross Macdonald) December 13, 1915—July 11, 1983)
Notable Novels/Characters
The Drowning Pool (1950), *The Doomsters (1958)*, Lew Archer

Walter Mosley (January 12, 1952)
Notable Novels/Characters
Six Easy Pieces (2003), Easy Rawlins, Mouse
Fear Itself (2003), Fearless Jones
The Long Fall (2009), Leonid McGill

Georgiana Ann Randolph Craig (as Craig Rice, 1908—1957)
Notable Novels/Characters
The Wrong Murder (1940), John J. Malone, Jake Justus
The Sunday Pigeon Murders (1942), Bingo Riggs, Handsome Kusak

Mickey Spillane (March 9, 1918—July 17, 2006)
Notable Novels/Characters
I, the Jury (1947), Mike Hammer, Velda
Bloody Sunrise (1965), Tiger Mann
The Delta Factor (1968), Morgan the Raider

Cornell Woolrich (December 4, 1903—September 25, 1968)
Notable Novels/Characters
The Bride Wore Black (1940), Julie Killeen
The Black Angel (1943), Alberta "Angel Face" Murray
Night has a Thousand Eyes (as George Hopley, 1949), Tom Shawn

Appendix Two

Fabulous Femme Fatales

Along with gangsters, torpedoes, molls, and dicks, no classic crime caper is complete without a femme fatale. These seductive, mysterious ladies have been devouring men since ancient times, from Circe to Salome, on through the Roaring 20s and beyond. Some would argue these irresistible dames are the most essential piece of any hard-boiled tale. On the following pages you'll find a selection of women from the silver screen who have come to define the modern femme fatale.

WANTED
DEPARTMENT OF DAMES

VITALS

Born, Died: 1924-2014
Height: 5' 8.5"
Build: Slim
Hair: Light brown
Eyes: Hazel
Notable Appearances: The Big Sleep, To Have and Have Not, Key Largo, Dark Passage

LAUREN BACALL
ALIAS: Born Betty Joan Perske, AKA Kid AKA Slim AKA "The Look"

Record:
Sullen, sultry and sassy, Bacall's sex appeal and chemistry with Humphrey Bogart cemented her identity as the Grand Dame of noir. Her trademark gaze wasn't a calculated move, as she once explained, "I used to tremble from nerves so badly that the only way I could hold my head steady was to lower my chin practically to my chest and look up at Bogie. That was the beginning of 'The Look'" Engaged in an affair with Bogart who was 25 years her senior until his death 13 years later.

WANTED
DEPARTMENT OF DAMES

VITALS

Born, Died: 1902-1992
Height: 5' 5"
Build: 36-26-33
Hair: Blonde
Eyes: Blue
Notable Appearances: Shanghai Express, Witness for the Prosecution, Touch of Evil

Marlene Dietrich
Born Marie Magdalene Dietrich
AKA "Lily Marlene"

Record:
Held both American and German citizenship. Sexually ambiguous, glamorous, mysterious, but undeniably alluring to men (and women). Dietrich really didn't care what others thought; she was comfortable, if not downright sexy, in everything from gowns to trousers, tuxedos, and other masculine accoutrement. Dietrich knew her stuff, as she once said: "Darling, the legs aren't so beautiful, I just know what to do with them." Half of the earliest known girl on girl kiss in cinema ("Morocco," 1930). Refused to work in Germany under Nazi rule. Awarded the War Department's Medal of Freedom in 1947 for her volunteer work during the war effort.

WANTED
DEPARTMENT OF DAMES

VITALS

Born, Died: 1922-1990
Height: 5' 6"
Build: Hourglass
Hair: Auburn
Eyes: Green
Notable Appearances: The Killers, The Bribe, Singapore

Ava Gardner
Born Ava Lavinia Gardner AKA Snowdrop AKA Angel AKA The Christmas Eve Girl

Record:
Oozing enough sex appeal to incite any man to acts of desperation, Ava Gardner blasted into the femme fatale firmament in "The Killers." After marrying Mickey Rooney, Howard Hughes and Artie Shaw, she was the inamorata who broke up Frank Sinatra's marriage. Despite her own multiple marriages and "Other Woman" status, she had this to say, "Because I was promoted as a sort of a siren and played all those sexy broads, people made the mistake of thinking I was like that off the screen." You gotta love any woman who tosses around the term "broads."

WANTED
DEPARTMENT OF DAMES

VITALS

Born, Died: 1923-1981
Height: 5' 6"
Build: Just right
Hair: Blonde
Eyes: Hazel
Notable Appearances: In a Lonely Place, Sudden Fear, The Big Heat, Crossfire, Man on a Tightrope, Naked Alibi

Gloria Grahame
Alias: Born Gloria Hallward
AKA The Lip

Record:
Underneath her hard-bitten good looks and pouty come-hither lips lurked the face of the girl next door gone bad. Grahame's turn as the sexy yet sad Violet in "It's a Wonderful Life" aroused both lust and pity. She went on to portray a series of memorable femme fatales while showing off some serious acting chops, winning a best supporting actress Oscar for nine minutes of screen time in "The Bad and the Beautiful." Grahame's career sadly went off the rails due to a poisonous cocktail of scandalous private life and several less-than-successful plastic surgeries. Allegedly assaulted costars Charlotte Greenwood and Gene Nelson during the filming of "Oklahoma." Married four times, she had an affair with her teenage stepson who she later married. Ado Annie indeed.

WANTED
DEPARTMENT OF DAMES

VITALS

Born, Died: 1918-1987
Height: 5' 6"
Build: Stacked
Hair: Red
Eyes: Light Brown
Notable
Appearances: Blood and Sand, Gilda, The Lady from Shanghai

Rita Hayworth
Alias: Margarita Cansino, AKA The Love Goddess

Record:
A true sigh-reen of the silver screen. Rita Hayworth was married five times, counting Orson Welles and the son of the Aga Khan amongst her harem of ex-husbands. Accidentally knocked out two of Glenn Ford's teeth filming their brawl in "Gilda." First choice for the lead in "Casablanca" and one of the inspirations for Jessica Rabbit. Her smoky looks landed her on the cover of LIFE magazine five times and she had the number two pinup poster in WWII. Her legacy lives on beyond her big screen fame. Though she died of Alzheimer's disease, the annual Rita Hayworth Gala has raised more than 75 million simoleans for the Alzheimer's Association. A great legacy for a great dame.

WANTED
DEPARTMENT OF DAMES

VITALS

Born, Died: 1922-1973
Height: 4' 11"
Build: Slim and provocative
Hair: Blonde
Eyes: Blue
Notable
Appearances: The Blue Dahlia, This Gun for Hire, The Glass Key, Saigon

Veronica Lake
Alias: Born Constance Frances Marie Ockleman, AKA Connie Keane AKA Connie de Toth AKA The Peek-a-boo Girl

Record:
A tiny figure with a huge presence. Her sultry eyes beckoned men to ruin from behind her trademark peek-a-boo hairstyle. More than just a pretty face, Veronica Lake was an accomplished aviatrix. She earned her pilot's license and even flew solo between Los Angeles and New York. Her life's path ended sadder than any screen role. Hampered by an addiction to hooch as well as lurking mental illness, she was arrested more than once for D&D. In 1962 she was found working as a cocktail waitress in New York and living at an all-women's hotel. As she once said, "I was always a rebel and probably could have got much farther had I changed my attitude." In 2004, some of Lake's ashes were reportedly found in a New York antique store. One final mystery from a lady with mystique.

WANTED
DEPARTMENT OF DAMES

VITALS

Born, Died: 1921-2008
Height: 5' 7"
Build: Shapely
Hair: Dirty blonde
Eyes: Brown
Notable
Appearances: Detour, Apology for Murder, The Last Crooked Mile

Ann Savage
Alias: Born Bernice Maxine Lyon

Record:
By all accounts a sweet dame, she still had a bit of a wild side. Layouts in Esquire made her a WWII pinup fave with the troops. Her sultry, dangerous looks left more than one moviegoer weak in the knees. Earned her pilot's license at 58 and competed successfully in speed racing. Acclaimed director Wim Wenders was a fan, calling her work "15 years ahead of its time." Film critic Barry Norman summed her up nicely as "sultry and sexy... a feline film noir star at its finest." In 2007, TIME magazine named her portrayal of Vera in "Detour" one of the Top 10 Movie Villains.

WANTED
DEPARTMENT OF DAMES

VITALS

Born, Died: 1922-2015
Height: 5' 6"
Build: Knee-weakening
Hair: Blonde
Eyes: Hazel
Notable Appearances: Dead Reckoning, Pitfall, Too Late for Tears.

Lizbeth Scott
Alias: Born Emma Matzo AKA Scotty AKA "The Threat"

Record:
Her trademark husky voice was the perfect complement to her intense eyes and treacherous beauty. Often referred to as the most beautiful face of film noir, Lizbeth Scott was no second-stringer. It's claimed no other actress appeared in more noir films, and she was the leading lady in 22 of her 23 appearances.

At one point Scotty was dogged by rumors of lesbianism and prostitution by the yellow press. The scandal rag Confidential tried to shake her down by threatening to publish a salacious article if she didn't come up with some dough. You don't push a dame like "The Threat" around though, and she told them where to go. Confidential published the article "Lizabeth Scott in the Call Girls' Call Book" and Scott promptly sued for millions. The case ended in a mistrial. Confidential, however, was never the same after having the lie put to its stories thanks to Scott and eventually went belly up.

WANTED
DEPARTMENT OF DAMES

VITALS

Born, Died: 1907-1990
Height: 5' 5"
Build: 34-23-33
Hair: Blonde, dyed red
Eyes: Blue
Notable Appearances: Double Indemnity, The Strange Love of Martha Ivers, Clash by Night, The Two Mrs. Carrolls, Crime of Passion.

Barbara Stanwyck
Alias: Born Ruby Catherine Stevens AKA Missy AKA The Queen AKA Babs

Record:
Known for her sexy deep voice, Stanwyck's wicked turn as Phyllis Dietrichson in "Double Indemnity" was ranked #8 on the American Film Institute's "100 Greatest Screen Heroes and Villains" list (she was the villain). One critic described her performances as "a stirring mixture of toughness and sentiment, a truly creative and two-faced woman." She was orphaned at the age of four but fought her way up from Ziegfeld Girl to screen icon. Stanwyck was also a fan of Ayn Rand. At the age of 45 Babs hooked up with baby-faced 22-year-old up and comer Robert Wagner for several years. In an incident right out of a film noir, she was conked on the coconut by a sneak thief who made off with 40 large worth of ice from her Beverly Hills digs.

WANTED
DEPARTMENT OF DAMES

VITALS

Born, Died: 1921-1995
Height: 5' 3"
Build: Va-va-voom
Hair: Blonde
Eyes: Green
Notable
Appearances: The Postman Always Rings Twice, They Won't Forget, Johnny Eager

Lana Turner
Alias: Born Julia Jean Mildred Frances Turner AKA Judy AKA "The Sweater Girl"

Record:

Sexy, suggestive, and erotic, Lana Turner was a force to be reckoned with on screen. Off screen her personal life seemed to mirror her movie roles. Her father was murdered when she was a young girl. To raise money for bonds during World War II she began selling kisses to the largest bond buyers (anything for the war, right?) Turner was married and divorced eight times, twice to her first husband. She had an abusive relationship with gangster Johnny Stompanato, which was summarily dissolved when her teenage daughter shivved him in the gut during one of his violent outbursts with her mother. Lana Turner's role as the seductress in "The Postman Always Rings Twice" is often cited as the gold standard for femme fatales.

WANTED
DEPARTMENT OF DAMES

VITALS

Born, Died: 1919-2000
Height: 5' 9"
Build: Lithesome
Hair: Dark brown
Eyes: Hazel
Notable
Appearances: Force of Evil, The Narrow Margin, The Killing, The City that Never Sleeps.

Marie Windsor
Alias: Born Emily Marie Bertelsen

Record:
Almost other-worldly sexy, Marie Windsor's dark allure promised all sorts of rewards to the right man. Windsor used her gifts to the fullest, owning any role as temptress or villain. As described in The Narrow Margin, "She's a dish. A 60-cent special: cheap, flashy, strictly poison under the gravy." Apparently, she was a lady of many talents. She earned her way into Hollywood writing jokes for Jack Benny. No, seriously. After retiring from acting she surfaced her talent as a painter and sculptor. No ditzy dame her, she also served as a director of the Screen Actors Guild for 25 years. While her roles as Edna Tucker in "Force of Evil" and Sherry Peatty in "The Killing" are standouts, let's not forget her turn as the unwilling turncoat in "Cat-Women of the Moon!"

WANTED
DEPARTMENT OF DAMES

VITALS

Born, Died: 1905-1961
Height: 5' 6"
Build: Willowy
Hair: Black
Eyes: Brown
Notable
Appearances: Shanghai Express, Impact, Portrait in Black, Limehouse Blues.

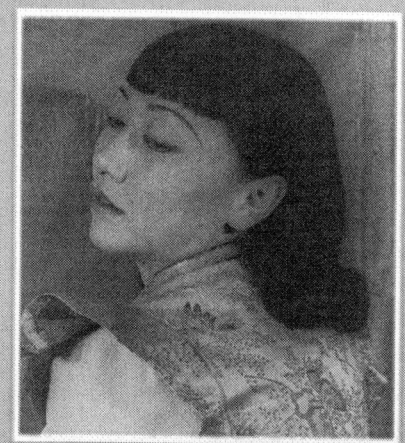

Anna May Wong
Alias: Born Wong Liu Tsong
AKA Bessie May Wong

Record:
Poised, talented, modern, beautiful, intelligent, dignified, classy, sexy, sophisticated, fearless, expressive. Anna May Wong was a major talent, one of the few actresses to successfully transition from silent pictures to talkies. She was the first Chinese-American to become a major box office attraction. Racial stereotyping often cast her as the "oriental siren," but her talent shown through in several memorable movies in Europe and the U.K. Wong had a nightclub act where she sang in French, German, English, and Chinese. Received third billing in "Shanghai Express." Her warm relationship with Cecil Cunningham and Marlene Dietrich led to rumors of sapphism. Seems a couple of dames couldn't hang out without tongues wagging. Most of Wong's movies are hard to come by, so if you find one for sale or streaming, don't pass it up — you won't be disappointed.

Appendix Three

Songs and Musical Artists to Put You in a Mobstery Mood.

Spanning the Jazz Era through modern-day artists, enjoy my playlist on an ebon eve when the rain cuts through the night like a betrayed wife's butcher knife.

SINGLES

Ain't Gonna Drown – Elle King

All the Same to Me – Anya Marina

Cry Me a River – Julie London

Fever – Peggy Lee

God Bless the Child – Billie Holliday

Harlem Nocturne – The Viscounts or the Max Gregor version

I Got it Bad (and That Ain't Good) – Nina Simone

I've Got to See You Again – Norah Jones

In the Air Tonight – Phil Collins

It's Easy to Remember – John Coltrane

Knock 1,2, 3 – Imelda May

La Vie En Rose – Edith Piaf or Louse Armstrong

Looks that Kill – Shivaree

Meet You at the Moon – Imelda May

Minnie the Moocher – Cab Calloway or Big Bad Voodoo Daddy

My One and Only Thrill – Melody Gardot

Nasty, Naughty Boy – Christina Aguilera

Passion Flower – Grover Washington, Jr.

Queen of Pain – Devil Doll

Satin Doll – Johnny Hodges

Second Chance – Paul Gonslaves

Secret (Two Can Keep a Secret, if One of Them is Dead) – The Pierces

Smoker's Song – Imelda May

Stella by Starlight – Tony Lakotos

The Other Woman – Caro Emerald

The Peter Gunn Theme – Henry Mancini

Theme for Ernie – John Coltrane

Tom's Diner – Suzanne Vega and DNA

What if I Leave – Rachael Yamagata

Your Heart is Black as the Night – Melody Gardot

ALBUMS

Drink Up Light Up – Various Artists

Jazz Noire: Darktown Sleaze from The Mean Streets of 1940's L.A. – Various Artists

Jazz Noir: 60 Menacing Masterpieces – Various Artists

Mingus Ah Um – Charles Mingus

Music to Make Love to Your Old Lady By – Lovage

Queen of Pain – Devil Doll

The Shocking Miss Emerald – Caro Emerald

Wise Guys and Wild Women – Various Artists

Appendix Four

Suggestions for a Film Noir Binge-Watch Queue

The only thing better than a good old, hard-boiled detective story is a hard-boiled film. Presented here without comment is a list, spanning the beginning of the film industry through modern times, of some personal favorites and genre milestones.

Anatomy of a Murder (1959)

Blood Simple (1984)

Blue Velvet (1986)

Body Double (1984)

Body Heat (1981)

Chinatown (1974)

Detour (1945)

Devil in a Blue Dress (1995)

Double Indemnity (1944)

Gilda (1946)

The Glass Key (Both the 1935 and 1942 versions are good)

In a Lonely Place (1950)

Key Largo (1948)

Kiss Me Deadly (1955)

Lady from Shanghai (1947)

Laura (1944)

LIttle Caesar (1931)

Mulholland Drive (2001)

Murder My Sweet (1944)

My Gun is Quick (1957)

Out of the Past (1947)

Scarface (1932)

Sin City (2005)

The Big Heat (1953)

The Big Sleep (1946)

The Killers (1946)

The Maltese Falcon (1941)

The Postman Always Rings Twice (1946 version)

The Public Enemy (1931)

The Thin Man (1934)

The Third Man (1949)

Too Late for Tears (1949)

Touch of Evil (1958)

White Heat (1949)

About The Author

Throughout his career Joe Tradii has won a heap of awards as a copywriter and published thought leadership articles on brand and marketing management. He has taught and lectured on marketing and branding strategy at Seattle University, City University, and other braineries.

He lives and continues to write in North Bend, Washington with his wife Cheryl and their jamoke of a cat Wesley, who has shown a distinct antipathy toward him (the cat, not the wife).

Visit facebook.com/GuysMolls
to participate in contests,
discussions and more!

What words or expressions would
you like to see in Volume II?

email ameche2zozzled@gmail.com
with your suggestions.

Credits
Cover photo © Bruno Passigattis, stock.adobe.com
Appendix One photo © fresnel6, stock.adobe.com
Appendix Two photo: © pauldimarco, stock.adobe.com
Photos of Lauren Bacall et al public domain. Photo of Anna May Wong by Carl Van Vechten, public domain.
Appendix Three photo © James Steidl, adobe.stock.com
Appendix four photo © socialogas, adobe.stock.com
Back cover photo: © cherylvb, stock.adobe.com

Every effort has been made to trace the copyright holders and obtain permission to reproduce any copyrighted material. Any omission will be corrected in later editions.

Made in the USA
Lexington, KY
22 January 2019